I Remember
TED WILLIAMS

Other Books in the I Remember Series

I Remember
TED WILLIAMS

*Anecdotes and Memories of Baseball's
Splendid Splinter by the Players and
People Who Knew Him*

DAVID CATANEO

CUMBERLAND HOUSE
NASHVILLE, TENNESSEE

Published by Cumberland House Publishing, Inc., 431 Harding Industrial
Drive, Nashville, TN 37211

Cover design by Gore Studio, Inc.
Text design by Mary Sanford

Library of Congress Cataloging-in-Publication Data

Cataneo, David.
   I remember Ted Williams : anecdotes and memories of baseball's
Splendid Splinter by the players and people who knew him / David
Cataneo.
      p. cm.
   Includes index.
   ISBN 1-58182-249-9 (alk. paper)
   1. Williams, Ted, 1918– —Anecdotes. 2. Williams, Ted, 1918– —
Friends and associates. 3. Baseball players—United States—
Biography. I. Title.
   GV865.W5 C38 2002
   795.357'092—dc21
   [B]   2001058220

Printed in the United States of America

2 3 4 5 6 7 8 9 10—06 05 04 03 02

For H.W.C.,
the greatest mom who ever lived

Contents

Acknowledgments

Thanks to all who shared memories of Ted Williams:

Bobby Doerr, Johnny Pesky, Boo Ferriss, Mel Parnell, Johnny Sain, Bobby Knight, Tony Lupien, Eddie Joost, Autumn Durst Keltner, Joe Villarino, Sam Mele, Maureen Cronin, Matt Batts, Eldon Auker, George Scott, Dick Bosman, Jerry Coleman, Red Auerbach, Dee Haynes, Sam Chapman, Max West, Les Cassie Jr., Don Mincher, Bob Breitbard, Ray Boone, Mickey Vernon, Dario Lodigiani, Ed Penney, Tom Ross, Ed Buchser, Woody Woodbury, Larry Hawkins, Frank Cushing, Frank Malzone, Chuck Stevens, and Charlie Wagner.

Special thanks to two mentors and masters, George Sullivan and Tim Horgan.

Thank you, Jim Gallagher, E. B. Cataneo, Crystal Hubbard, Nancy Purbeck, Ocie Cataneo, Emil Sitka, Randy

Farley, Tinn Thuddywan, and especially to Dick Beverage and Patty Helmsworth.

Finally, my gratitude to Mike Towle, Ed Curtis, and Ron Pitkin for their support and guidance.

INTRODUCTION

No one crosses paths with Ted Williams and forgets about it. Who could forget Paul Bunyan?

So it was good fun to round up fishing buddies, hunting cronies, former ballplayers, former marines, and long-time pals for this little book. Asking people to talk about Ted is like asking them to talk about their kids: They'll go on and on about how the little ones are talented, smart, generous, sometimes funny, sometimes petty, sometimes unbearable, but ultimately the best in the world. And a lot of people did offer to show me snapshots.

I first met Ted Williams in 1989 on a hot summer morning in Cooperstown, New York. It was the day after Carl Yastrzemski and others had been bronzed at the Hall of Fame. Now a collection of classic all-time baseball heroes, in town for the ceremony, were gathered in a function room to meet the press. Each round table featured a wrinkly legend, but for me—a baseball writer from Boston—there was only one place to go.

Ted's table was filled. He leaned back in his plastic chair, put his hand on his chin, squinted down his nose at us, and waited for questions. We clicked our pens, rustled our notepads, fiddled with our tape recorders, but no one said a word.

I think we were intimidated. We were young "knights of the keyboard," and here was the most famous fire-breathing jouster in baseball history. Many of us had heard all about him from our ink-stained, fedora-wearing mentors: He tormented sportswriters the way little boys torment frogs. On Ted's list of loathsome persons, reporters were way below pitchers and slightly above Alger Hiss.

At age seventy, Ted was still big and loud. If he needed to, he still looked plenty rugged enough to crush a fastball into the bleachers, yank a tarpon out of teal water, shotgun a duck on the wing, dead-stick a flaming fighter jet on a runway, or chase a sportswriter out of a clubhouse. Or out of a function room at the Hall of Fame.

We stared at Ted Willams. He stared back.

He stroked his chin, smiled slightly, and said with his well-known, playfully sarcastic growl, "Scared to death, huh?"

The questions started, and we were introduced to a lesser-known fact about Ted Williams and the press: He was a terrific interview. He was bright, clever, informed, articulate. We only talked baseball but got the impression we could have asked him about the Treaty of Versailles, or about chili recipes, or about the principal exports of New Zealand, and he would have delivered a strong, informed opinion about it. Or at least he would have been willing to run out and get one.

I asked him about the time he discussed the science of hitting with Ty Cobb.

"Yeaaaah, I talked to him about it," Ted said. He recounted Cobb's approach as opposed to his approach. Then he boomed, "And I still KNOW that I was RIGHT!"

And at that moment, I became a Ted Williams admirer. I never saw him play, I was not a native New Englander, I never bought fishing tackle from Sears. But anyone who conjured passion and exclamation points about a four-decade-old conversation was okay.

Ted Williams left an impression, beyond a ringing in my ears.

That's what this book is about—impressions of Ted Williams. This is not a last-word biography. It's a stroll through his life with his friends, his teammates, and other onlookers. It is a chance to sit back, as if you were in a baseball dugout on a warm afternoon, or in front of a fireplace on a cold night, and hear tall tales and medium tales and short tales of Ted Williams, his legend, his exploits, his follies, and his blue ox, Babe.

I Remember
TED WILLIAMS

THUMPING THEODORE

He had two lockers. One for him. One for his bats.
—RED SOX INFIELDER EDDIE JOOST

Whenever Ted Williams stepped to the plate, everybody stopped. Ballplayers stopped spitting on the floor and scratching at their flannel. Ushers stopped ushering. Fans stopped calling for the hot-dog man.

Ted at bat was one of the great masterworks of twentieth-century America, four times per game. He perfected the art. Ella sang, Picasso painted, Hemingway typed, Tracy acted, the Three Stooges threw pies. Ted hit. Nobody wanted to miss that.

"You had to watch this guy," said Chuck Stevens, who played first base for the St. Louis Browns. "That's the thing I remember the most. Everybody watching. His contemporaries. His peers. Everybody. Watching him hit. You knew you were watching the best."

To Ted Williams, it was a mere matter of geometry, physics, and will. He was a great hitter because he decided he would be. At age twelve, he thought it would be neat to grow up to be a .400 hitter, and he got to work on it. Ted Williams often said that he wanted to be remembered as the greatest hitter who ever lived, and he just did it.

He was good in math: Ted hit .406 in 1941, .388 at age thirty-nine, and won a batting title at forty. Lifetime, he batted .344 with 521 home runs, and he could have had 700 homers if not for the four seasons lost to two wars. With his Chuck Yeager eyesight and picky tastes, he walked 2,019 times and struck out 709 times.

He was good in art: Ted Williams's lefty swing was sweet and beautiful.

His hitting landed him some cool nicknames—the Splendid Splinter, Thumper—and also landed him on every fantasy team. You might want to go back in time to watch Willie Mays and Joe DiMaggio play baseball, but you'd go back to watch Ted Williams swing a bat.

You think about Ted when you watch *The Natural*, but he was more than a born hitter. He was born to hit. No one studied, examined, practiced, dissected, or enjoyed hitting more than Ted did. It was the love of his life. Joe had Marilyn. Ted had hitting.

"It never left his mind," former teammate Birdie Tebbetts said.

His physical skills were legendary. He had 20-10 vision—he claimed he could see the ball flatten as it hit the bat. He had startling, quick reflexes—he claimed he could smell wood burn from friction after a vicious foul tip.

But his devotion was the bigger legend. He used his school lunch money to pay kids to pitch to him. He weighed his bats at the post office. He practiced hitting everywhere. He asked and mused about hitting endlessly; when he sat in preflight school studying aerodynamics, he applied it to the spin of curve balls and the effect of wind on fly balls.

As a young man, he gazed at shooting stars and wished "that someday I could be the hitter I always wanted to be." As an old man, he dreamed that he was batting against Randy Johnson (Ted singled up the middle).

In 1970, he wrote a book about his grand passion. He titled it *The Science of Hitting,* which only proved that he was no Robert Browning.

Ted was head over heels about hitting, and they were a beautiful couple. For nineteen summers, New Englanders lived for his next at bat. When he stepped to the plate, no one stepped away from the box seat, the bleacher, the radio, or the television. The next beer could wait.

Something unforgettable was happening.

"One day, I interviewed a blind guy at Fenway Park," long-time *Boston Herald* columnist Tim Horgan said. "I said to him, 'If you pardon me, why do you come to the park?'

"He said, 'It's the sounds at the park. For instance, I can always tell when Ted Williams is doing anything. Because there's a whole tension in the park. I can tell when he gets off the bench in the dugout and gets his bat and starts up the steps. Just by the sounds in the park. The whole place comes alive. When he comes to the plate, everybody's up.'"

Joe Villarino, Ted's childhood pal in San Diego:

He lived on Utah Street and I lived on Oregon Street. We went to Garfield Grammar School. In order to get to school, he'd walk to my house, and we'd walk together to the school, which was only about a half block away.

We used to get there early in the morning. They had a box there that had all the bats and the balls and the volley-balls and such. Ted would always be the first one there to get the ball and the bat out. He just loved to hit that ball.

In those days, they just played one game a week, on Fridays. They had a short right-field fence. Ted, you know how he could hit 'em. He'd hit 'em nine miles over that fence.

Well, he batted fourth and I batted fifth. He hit this long home run—I guess the ball is still rolling. And I hit one right after him, and it just barely went over the fence. And Ted was waiting for me there at the plate. He said, "Man, that was the longest ball you hit in a long time. And it just barely went over the fence."

We used to hang around the playground. We played this game called "Big League." It was kind of a converted hand-ball court. It had these pipes that ran along there. If you hit this one pipe parallel to the ground, it was a home run. Ted was awful good at that. He just loved to hit. We did that in junior high quite a bit.

He always wanted to play. He loved being out there on the diamond. I'd pitch to him and shag fly balls for him. There was a guy by the name of Rod Luscomb. He was the playground director. Rod would pitch to him, and I would chase balls for him. They used to go over a fence in right field and land in a neighbor's yard across the street.

He didn't like to go to movies too much. The only time he liked to go was when Olivia de Havilland was playing. He loved Olivia de Havilland. He didn't go too much, because he was afraid of hurting his eyes.

He loved to eat. Anything. There was a malt shop right across the street from Hoover High School. It was a drugstore with a soda fountain. Malted milk and ice-cream cones. We used to go over there quite a bit. Ted loved milk shakes. He never did drink beer or anything. He never smoked. He was full of energy. Always on the go. But most of all, he loved to hit. He was always trying to get somebody to pitch to him.

Hoover High classmate **Les Cassie Jr.:**

We started practice just before the semesters changed in 1934. All of the guys who were going out for baseball were out there. We had a lot of kids out for baseball.

Wos Caldwell was our coach. He was conducting practice. We were out in a big field, just a blank piece of ground between the stadium and the school. It was a big piece of ground. In what would have been right field if it was a ballpark, was the lunch arbor where we all ate our lunches. There was a series of benches and tables with a roof over them. This would have been deep right field.

Well, it was getting late in practice. A tall, skinny kid came walking down the walk right in front of the shops. He sat down on the steps of the print shop. He finally said, "Hey, Coach. Let me hit." Caldwell didn't know him from Adam. Nor did anybody else.

Caldwell didn't pay any attention to him. He was concerned about all the kids he had out there wanting to play for Hoover. So Ted just sat there for another twenty or thirty minutes.

So finally he said a second time, "Coach, let me hit."

Caldwell says, "Okay, get up there."

By this time, Caldwell was pitching batting practice himself. He had run out of batting practice pitchers. The first ball that Caldwell threw him, Ted hit it up on this lunch arbor. There was no other guy who had any ball near it.

He threw him another pitch, and it went up on the roof.

Caldwell says, "What's your name, kid?"

He says, "My name's Ted Williams, and I'll be here next Monday."

We just seemed to become friends. We used to eat lunch together. We'd take our brown bags and sit on the steps of the auditorium and eat our lunch. When we were sitting on the steps eating our lunch, I can still remember him, he was sitting there and he kind of had a short-sleeved shirt on and he rolled up the sleeves. And he said, "This is what I want to do. I want to roll up my sleeves and hit the ball so hard that everybody will say that I'm the best hitter who ever was." He was a sixteen-year-old kid, and that was in his mind.

Baseball. That's all he was interested in. I think that's been true all his life. Everything he did practically was aimed at being a great hitter. All his spare time was spent at the playground, swinging a bat. A lot of people would pitch to him. A fella by the name of Wilbur Wiley, mostly. Wilbur pitched more batting practice to Ted than any other bunch of guys. Ted was a worker. There's no doubt in my mind that his primary goal in life was to hit.

We used to try to get heavier. Both of us. We couldn't gain a pound. We'd have milk shakes and stuff. He worked at gaining strength in his arms. He knew it was important to be strong in the arms to be a good hitter. He would get down on all fours and lift the dining room chair off the floor with one hand and then the other. At his house. And they were heavy chairs. I couldn't do it.

San Diego native and major-league infielder **Ray Boone:**

There were about eight of us in the neighborhood. We never missed watching Ted play on Friday when he was in high school. If you missed the game, you called your buddy. And he'd always say, "You should have been there. You missed it. Ted hit one of those eucalyptus trees out there."

Whenever we saw him, whether it was in a theater or something, we were awed by him. That's how good he was. I used to tell Ted, when I played with him on the Red Sox in 1960, that he was a better hitter in high school than he was in the big leagues.

He was so tall and gangly and skinny. He had so much flexibility in his swing. We all admired that swing. We wished we had that same ability.

Del Ballinger lived right next door to me. Del was probably my mentor. Every Saturday, Del was painting shinguards, or doing something that had to do with baseball. He told me one day, "Ted's coming over here tomorrow about ten o'clock." I said, "Can I tell my friends?" Del said, "Sure."

So about five of us showed up. When Ted came over, Del was out there on the porch. Del called us over. So I got to meet Ted. It was just like meeting the president of the United States.

Chuck Stevens, *first baseman for the St. Louis Browns, 1946, 1948:*

At that time, Vern Stephens and I were at Long Beach Poly. We were all playing ball. There was a club called the 20-30 Club. They promoted business knowledge and public speaking and that sort of thing. A 20-30 Club in Pomona promoted a baseball tournament to be played during the Easter week vacation. This would have been in 1936.

They invited schools from all over. Poly was invited. Hoover was invited. We heard there was somebody down there, a big tall guy, that could really play. But we never paid much attention to it, because Pasadena Tech had a guy by the name of Jackie Robinson in the tournament, and we heard he was a pretty good ballplayer, too.

We go to Pomona. This is a massive ball field. There are two or three diamonds out there where they could play ball games at the same time—one in the far corner, one in the far corner. We're on one of them in one of the far corners and we're playing Jackie Robinson's ball club. And way down on the other far corner is a ball game. We don't know who's playing down there. But sometime during the ball game, we're in the field. And an umpire calls time out. And a baseball rolls through our infield from behind us. We get the baseball and turn around to see what's going on. And there's that big, long, lanky, loping stride going around the bases in the far corner.

We later found out who in the world hit THAT. It was Ted Williams.

Hoover chum **Bob Breitbard:**

This guy just loved baseball so much that he played baseball all year around. He went to the North Park playgrounds and hit baseballs. He had a fella there by the name of Rod Luscomb, who just idolized Ted. He was kind of Ted's mentor. They played baseball. All year around, that's what he did.

Ted could have gone to Hoover High School or to San Diego High School. We were on the borderline. San Diego High School had a great baseball team. Had a great coach. But Ted selected Hoover High School because Ted didn't think he could make the club at San Diego High. He was playing for the varsity in 1934. Now, he played in the '34 season, the '35 season, and the '36 season. So at the end of the '36 season, he didn't have any more eligibility for baseball.

He signed with the Padres in the Pacific Coast League. So he was playing for the Padres while he was still in high school.

He always said that he wanted to be a professional baseball player. In our yearbook, it says: "What do you want to do?" He just put—he didn't say professional baseball—he just put "baseball." That's all.

He always wanted to be known as the greatest hitter who ever lived.

Hall of Famer **Bobby Doerr,** *a long-time pal and Ted's teammate on the San Diego Padres, as well as the Boston Red Sox, 1939–44, 1946–51:*

I was with the Padres. In June, we're standing by the batting cage and I'm standing on the right side of the cage. All the players were around that old-style batting cage that we used to have. And right in front of me was standing Ted Williams. At that time, he was about 147 pounds and six-foot-three. A tall, skinny kid. Nobody knew who he was.

Frank Shellenback was the manager of the team. He was pitching batting practice that day. He yelled in, "Let's see the kid get in and hit a few." All the players were around the cage, ex-major-leaguers and such. You could hear them grumbling, "Oh, geez, this guy is going to take up all our time in batting practice." They were grunting and groaning.

Ted had six or seven balls to hit. Most of them were line drives. I think he might have hit one out of the park and one against the fence. We didn't even have players who could hit the fence. We didn't have that kind of power. He really made an impression.

I can always remember a player over on the third-base side of the batting cage saying, "This kid will be signed before the week is out." That was on a Thursday. Every Monday was an off day in the Coast League in those days. We were taking the train to San Francisco to play the Seals or the Missions. When we went down to the depot that night, well here's Ted, prancing up and down the side of the train. He was all excited. They had signed him. I think he got something like a $125- or $150-a-month contract.

The Kid at bat was special, and smart baseball people knew it right away. **Ray Boone:**

Herb Benninghaven was a part-time scout for the St. Louis Cardinals. He worked for the San Diego Gas Company. He always had a Sunday ball club. A lot of those guys played for him on Sunday. As a scout, it was a way for him to get to know different prospects. Ted used to hang out at his house all the time. They only lived a few doors apart and he would always come over. Herb's wife was always cooking and baking.

When Ted was . . . ready to sign . . . , he signed with the Padres for $800. Ted told Herb that if he could get him $1,000, he would sign with the Cardinals. Herb said yes, he'd try to do it. Years later, Herb showed me the telegram from the Cardinals, rejecting his prospect—Ted Williams. The Cardinals could have had Williams and [Stan] Musial in the same outfield.

San Diego neighborhood squirt, **Frank Cushing:**

I grew up in Kensington, which is near Hoover High School, and Ted grew up in University Heights. I didn't know him at all, but I used to go over with a friend and we used to watch the Hoover baseball team practice. I used to shag balls over at Hoover High School for Ted when I was little. Of course, Ted had some notoriety then for being a big hitter.

In 1936, I was in the third grade when Ted was still in high school but playing for the San Diego Padres. The batboy who was selected for the Padres was a guy by the name of Ralph Thompson. During that summer, about seven of us in the third-grade class met Ted through Ralph Thompson.

Ralph said he would arrange after the game to introduce us to various players. That was a great big thrill. It was the first time I had ever met a professional athlete. And, of course, it was just a fleeting meeting. I shook his hand.

He was all of seventeen years old.

Johnny Pesky, *long-time friend and Red Sox infielder 1942, 1946–52:*

I was the clubhouse kid in Portland and he was with San Diego. That was the first time I ever saw him. He was electrifying then. And he was only a seventeen-, eighteen-year-old kid. He was a long, tall skinny guy. I don't think he weighed 160, 165 pounds. But he had a great swing. Oh, a great swing.

Ray Boone:

We'd go see Ted play with the Padres. All the time. We'd go down and hang out. Once the game started, any fly balls that came out of the park, if you brought the ball back, that would get you into the ball game free. So as soon as you got your ball, you and your buddies would block for the other guy. That caused a few ruckuses. We were down there to see the Padres, and to see Ted.

Autumn Durst Keltner, *daughter of Cedric Durst, who played outfield for the Padres after his major-league career:*

Dad was asked to work with him, but all Ted wanted to do was hit. That was the most important thing. Ted came in as a pitcher. Of course, with that hitting ability, he needed to get in the lineup more often.

They wanted him in the outfield, and Dad was a natural outfielder. So he worked with Ted a lot on his fielding. Dad talked a lot about that, and how Ted was not really interested in the fielding aspect. Although he was a quick study.

Eddie Joost, *major-league infielder 1936–55:*

He was in the Coast League when I was in the Coast League. I was with the old Missions. I saw him when he came up to San Francisco to play.

We were amazed just watching him in batting practice. He looked like he weighed maybe 146 pounds. A real slim guy. But in batting practice, he was hitting balls over the fence 360 feet away in right field.

This guy had the perfect swing, which he had all his life.

Dario Lodigiani, *who played infield for the Pacific Coast League's Oakland Oaks, the Philadelphia Athletics, and later the Chicago White Sox:*

I remember he was a big, tall, skinny guy. And Lefty O'Doul, who was the manager of the San Francisco Seals, saw him for the first time. Lefty, you know, led the National League in hitting twice. He was the kind of guy who was a great hitting instructor. And he told Ted Williams, who was just out of high school, "Kid, I'm going to tell you something. Don't you ever let anybody mess around with your swing. Right now, it's almost perfect."

I remember when he said that.

Les Cassie Jr.:

He was a pretty good pitcher. He broke into the Coast League as a pitcher. After the Padres signed him, they were playing in Los Angeles one night and he hadn't gotten into a game yet. They were getting beat bad, so they put Ted in to pitch. I'm not sure I got the details right, but I think he got the first guy out. And the next guy hit a triple off the fence. And then he got a guy out, which was the third out. Then I'll be darned, his turn at bat came up after that inning and he got a double. He could hit. He was outstanding. He was better than anyone else.

So they put him in left field and left him there for the rest of the ball game. My dad and I were listening to that game over the radio.

Eddie Collins of the Red Sox succeeded where Herb Benninghaven of the Cardinals failed. **Bobby Doerr:**

Ted really didn't play that much the first part of the season. He mostly took batting practice and such.

In the winter of '35, the Red Sox had taken an option to buy George Myatt, who was the shortstop, and me as the second base–shortstop combination. They were supposed to decide in the middle of the year in '36 whether they were going to exercise the option on us. Either one of us or both of us.

In '36, we were playing up in the Northwest, Seattle and Portland. I didn't know it at the time, but Collins had been watching us. It was on a double-header Sunday that somebody said that Eddie Collins was in the stands. Well, my gosh. In those days, you never saw a scout. I knew he was deciding about it. I made three errors in the game. You just got nervous.

In between games, he knocks on the door of the club-house. He said he wanted to see me. He said that the Red Sox were going to take my contract, but not Myatt's. They had Joe Cronin as the shortstop and they didn't need another shortstop. But he had seen Ted taking batting practice. I don't think Ted got into a game at that time.

Collins evidently went down to San Diego to see Bill Lane, who was the owner of the Padres to see if the Red Sox could buy Ted's contract. The story I got was that Lane said not at that time, because they wanted to see what Ted could do. Collins had the foresight to ask if the Red Sox could have first chance to sign Ted when it came time to sell him. They shook hands on the deal.

In the winter meetings of 1937, that's when they decided they would go through with the deal. Ted had had that good year in 1937.

The Red Sox contacted Doerr and asked him to escort young Ted from California to Sarasota, Florida, for the Kid's first big-league spring training camp in 1938. Max West, who was reporting to the Boston Braves; former Brooklyn Dodger star Babe Herman, who was headed to a minor-league outpost somewhere; and Williams and Doerr all ended up on the same train. **Doerr:**

They had had flash floods that washed out the train tracks and knocked down the telephone wires and everything. I couldn't get ahold of Ted, and he couldn't get ahold of me. Ted had the foresight enough to get ahold of a ham operator

17

in San Diego to contact somebody in Los Angeles who got ahold of me.

We got on the train and went to El Paso. When we got to El Paso, we had about a three-hour layover. Babe Herman had been making these trips before. He said, "Let's go over to Juarez, Mexico. I know a place where we can get a good quail dinner." So we went over and had dinner. And when we come back, why, there again, prancing up and down alongside the train was Ted Williams.

It was on the train that Ted was pumping Babe Herman about hitting. Anyone that was a good hitter, Ted would quiz him about the different ideas of hitting.

One day in the Pullman, Ted got a pillow, and he was using the pillow as a bat. Ted was extremely loud with his talk, and a couple of women in the back of the car told the conductor, "We'd like you to try to keep that guy quiet." He was all excited being with Babe Herman.

Max West:

What I really remember about Ted was, I would open the window in the morning, when we were stopped. I would still be in bed. I would open the window and look out there, and there's Ted, walking up and down and balancing himself on the rails. He's walking up and down and balancing himself. And he's got a newspaper or a magazine in his hands, making like he's hitting a ball.

He's swinging and balancing himself on the railway. Every morning!

Williams was eventually farmed out to the Red Sox's top minor-league club, the Minneapolis Millers, but not before he had made an impression. **Doerr:**

When we got to Sarasota, we were supposed to report to Cronin. I introduced Ted to Joe. I said, "This is Ted." And Ted said to Joe, "Hi, sport." I think that might have been his ticket to Minneapolis.

I told Ted, "Wait until you see [Jimmie] Foxx hit some of these balls out of the park." He hit some like golf balls. Ted came back with, "Well, wait until they see me hit." He did say that.

Right-hander **Broadway Charlie Wagner,** *who pitched for the Red Sox 1938–42, 1946:*

He was a loner when he first broke in, in Minneapolis. And he hit like a son of a gun there, too. They had a short porch in right field. Ted hit them way out of there. Ted was hitting them into a restaurant out on the street. The guy was tired of putting windows in his place. Nobody else but Ted did that.

Ted was a little brash. He met Joe Cronin and he said, "Hiya, sport." But he wasn't a cocky guy. He just said little things. He was so intent. To begin with, he was as good a hitter as you'd ever want to see. You could hear the ring of the bat. I remember Donie Bush—he was my manager out in

Minneapolis. Donie Bush played with Ty Cobb. And he played against Shoeless Joe Jackson. And Eddie Collins, he played with Shoeless Joe Jackson. And they were talking one day, Mr. Bush and Mr. Collins. Ted was out there hitting at the time, in batting practice. They were comparing Ted to Shoeless Joe Jackson, and they agreed that Ted was as great as any hitter they had ever seen.

Ted studied hard under hitting coach Rogers Hornsby in Minneapolis and came back in the spring of 1939 to stick with the Red Sox. And the pesky, noisy craftsman went to work. **Charlie Wagner:**

I used to sit between Lefty Grove and Jimmie Foxx. Ted was always there at Jimmie Foxx's locker. "How do you hit this guy? How do you do this? How do you do that?" He was always questioning guys. Ted always thought Foxx was the greatest. He loved Foxx.

You got a kick out of Ted. Jimmie Foxx said, "He'll slow down. One of these days."

He was a young guy. He was talkative and so forth. They used to kid him. The big leaguers all did that. You had to understand him. And the more you were with Ted the more you understood him, if he had a little brash moment or something.

We had a great guy in Moe Berg. I used to hang with him a lot. They used to call me "Little Moe." No one is more fascinating than that guy. He and Ted talked all the time. Moe knew how to handle him. He soft-talked him. Moe used to do that crossword puzzle in the *New York Times* like he was writing a letter. I think Ted learned from these guys. You learned how. Ted would ask Moe questions like, "Gee, how about that Ted Lyons? How did he pitch? Did he almost come over the top?" He'd ask Moe a million questions. If Ted didn't know about something, he'd ask about it.

It was easy to be his roommate. He was baseball from morning to night. He studied it. He'd go to the room at night and study about who was going to pitch tomorrow. He didn't want to be second in anything he ever did. And he wasn't second, ever. His success came because he wanted to be first in everything. And he was first in everything.

Every day was a talk of something about baseball. Nothing else. He was so dedicated to his game of baseball, he never lifted anything else. Baseball was it.

He never wanted to be embarrassed at the plate. Ever. He talked about that. He said it. He said, "When I walk down the street, I want people to say, 'There goes Ted Williams, the best hitter I've ever seen.'" He said that to a lot of people. And here he was a young kid. I had nothing else to do but believe him.

Knuckleballers used to be a little threat to him. He used to tell you about this pitcher and about that pitcher. And he would go on and on and on. He could chew them up when he wanted to. And he always wanted to.

One day I came into the room. We were in St. Louis. He had just gotten some new bats. The minute I got in, he said, "Jesus, feel these goddamn bats." You know, he swore a lot.

He said, "Damn, these are the best bats. Look at them. Feel that son of a bitch."

I looked at the bats and I sat myself on the bed and I watched him. He was shaving some of the handles on them. The wood shavings were going all over my bed. That didn't bother him.

Then he looked in the mirror. They had post beds then. He's looking in the mirror and saying, "Je-sus Christ . . . Je-sus Christ. Boy, give me that bat. Boy."

Then he swung the bat at the knob of my bedpost and knocked my bed down. He knocked the post off my bed.

He said, "Hey, call 'em up and have them send up another bed." It was that simple.

He was hitting .382 one time, and somebody wrote an article about him: "When is he going to hit home runs?" And that annoyed him a little bit. But he got over that quickly and he told the guy about it on the train. He'd give the writers enough time, but he didn't want to be held up if it was baseball. If you'd come into the clubhouse, he was baseball every minute that he was in that clubhouse. And long before that, too.

He used to call me out of the dugout where they used to warm up before the game. "Hey, come over here a minute. I want to show you something. This is how I would pitch this guy. I'd give him the curve ball, the fastball, then I'd give him a changeup."

He'd talk about how he would pitch. On the last day of the year one year, Cronin said, "Well, I'm going to let him pitch today. One inning." It was against Detroit. Ted pitched. Hank Greenberg was hitting. Hank was a great hitter. One of the nice guys of all time. Hank hit one back through the box. Almost took Ted's head off.

Cronin says, "Oh, my God, I never thought about that." Hank broke two jaws with line drives. Fritz Ostermueller and Jimmie Wilson. Hank used to hit back through the middle. And he took him the hell out of there. Ted told me about this.

Ted got inside the pitcher's head. They used to throw at him when he first came up. You know, give him a shot under

The Kid. When he arrived in the big leagues, young Ted impressed and amused his teammates with nonstop chatter on the science of hitting.

the chin. But he saw the ball so well, he would just turn his head a little bit and he'd say, "Gee, that kid's wild today. He wasn't that wild before." He didn't think anybody would throw at him. And later on, they didn't. Why waken a sleeping dog? Besides, he saw the ball so well. I don't think you could hit him if you tried to hit him.

Eldon Auker, *the former Detroit Tiger star who pitched for the Red Sox in 1939:*

Ted was an excellent student of the game. He watched every pitcher that we faced. He'd be sitting on the bench and watching, and pretty soon he'd say, "You know, that pitcher

23

out there started the last four hitters out with a fastball." He'd be watching all the time, studying the pitcher.

In spring training, he drove everybody crazy asking us all about all the pitchers in the league. What kind of pitcher was he? How was his fastball? Was his best pitch the curve ball? What did he do when he was ahead of you? How did he pitch when he was behind? He just milked you dry.

Another thing—he asked all about the hitters. Did they pull the ball? Would they hit straight away? Did they go to the opposite field? Were they ground-ball hitters or fly-ball hitters? Or line-drive hitters or punch hitters? He just questioned you a-l-l-l-l the time.

In the clubhouse, we had a big mirror in there. We used it for dressing. He always had a bat in his hand, standing in front of that mirror. Dry-swinging. Watching his swing. Always studying his swing. All the time.

I don't think that year that he had a date with a girl. He was so tied up in what he was doing, so concentrated on what he was doing, and how the game was played in the major leagues. I never saw a coach or Joe Cronin, who was the manager, move Ted around in the outfield. Whoever was hitting, Ted would always move himself. That's because he studied the hitters. He just had a mind like a computer. Very, very sharp.

He didn't smoke. He didn't drink. He was in hog heaven, playing in the major leagues. He enjoyed it. You could just see it, how much he was enjoying it. Like a big kid, with a new toy.

He was out early in the mornings. He'd get out and take batting practice early and he'd just hit until game time. In the outfield, he was always running. He was always in perfect condition. He did that by running. He used to always want to throw a ball to a catcher so he could throw the ball hard. And he was always working on a knuckle ball. We used to kid him about that: "How's the knuckle ball today?"

I was with the St. Louis Browns in 1942. We were playing a ball game in Boston. It was the first year that Johnny Pesky came up with the Red Sox. I had [Lefty] Grove beat, 2-1, going into the ninth inning. All I had to do was get three men out.

Pesky dumped the first ball down the third-base line and beat it out. Ted was the next hitter.

Bobby Swift was my catcher. Bobby came out to me on the mound and said, "What do you think Ted will be doing? Think he'll be trying to tie up the game or will he be hitting straight away? What's he gonna do?"

I said, "Well, let's just keep the ball down and outside and see what he's going to do." So I threw a ball about six inches outside and about knee-high, and he hit it into the center-field stands like a two-iron. He beat me.

After he went around the bases and we were going into the dugout, in the runway going to the clubhouse, he was there waiting for me. He was laughing. I said, "You get away from me or I'm going to punch you in the nose." He said, "I know what you told Swift. You told him, 'Let's see what he's going to do. Let's keep it down and away from him.' You threw it exactly where I knew you were going to throw it. I was all ready for it."

That just shows how he was thinking. This guy had his head in the ball game all the time. He was thinking all the time.

Dario Lodigiani:

Ted lo-o-oved to talk about hitting. This was when we were in the big leagues. I remember in spring training, Ted would hold court. He would start talking about hitting, and pretty soon everybody would be around him. He would go right down to the fine points of hitting.

I asked him one time, "Ted, I have to ask you a question. Can you see that ball and the bat meet when you swing?" He said, "I see it a lot of the time." I told him he was full of crap. "Nobody can see that ball," I said. "It's a big blur right when it happens." He said, "No, sir." He looked at me in a convincing way. I believed him. He could see the ball and the bat together when he swung.

I was talking to Sam Chapman one day about this. He played outfield for the Athletics. He was my roommate when I was with Philadelphia. He told me about the time Mr. Mack intentionally walked Ted Williams with the bases loaded. He got Frankie Hayes's attention—Frankie Hayes was the catcher—and Mr. Mack said, "Put him on." Frank looked at him and said, "Mr. Mack, the bases are loaded." Mr. Mack said, "I know that. Put him on." They put him on.

The newspapermen asked Mr. Mack, "What was your thinking, walking him with the bases loaded?" Mr. Mack said, "I'd rather give him one run than four."

Johnny Pesky:

In my rookie year, we all lived over on Bay State Road. He lived at the old Sheraton. I know he had a bat up in his room and a big mirror. He'd swing in front of the mirror. He'd take some practice swings. He'd say something like, "We're in Detroit. Two men on. Two runs down and the Kid at bat.

"Pow! Over the fence!"

We had our own dining car, we had our own Pullman. He always held court. And he always had an audience. He'd give them situations. "What are you going to do with this guy? What are you going to do with that guy?" We talked baseball constantly.

Williams was always looking for that psychological edge. He could figure out a pitcher's thinking. He would just watch. He had a great mind, and that brought him to the next level. He always used to preach to us. "Get a good ball. When you get a good ball to hit—hit it!"

I'd be coming off the field and he'd say, "Come on, get your bat. Let's watch this guy." Especially if it was a new guy coming in from the bullpen. I remember when we first saw Whitey Ford. I was leading off the inning. He came in to relieve, to pitch to me and Williams. Ted says, "This guy has a pretty good reputation. Let's watch him warm up."

Spud Chandler was out in the Coast League when I was a clubhouse kid. He was out there because of an arm problem. He went out there so he could pitch a lot. He was always a good pitcher. I used to shine his shoes and hang up his uniform.

This is '42. Now I'm hitting at him in Boston. He was one of those guys who was very sour, dour. He was all business on the mound. We saw him once a series, every time we played the Yankees, and I couldn't hit him with a tennis racket. I was trying to pull the ball with him. I was trying to do something that I wasn't capable of, especially with a guy that threw that hard. He threw that hard sinker.

I was sitting in the dugout talking with a writer and he had his book out. We were looking at the stats. Ted was sitting on the bench a few feet away.

The writer said, "Johnny, you don't have a hit off of Chandler. You're 0-for-14." I said, "I couldn't be." Ted is sitting and he hears this. He comes over and says, "Yeah, for crying out loud. You're trying to pull this guy. You're just not strong enough. Your stroke is up the middle to left field, and you're trying to pull him. What are you trying to prove? I'm a foot taller and forty pounds heavier and I can't pull him."

I go, "Yeah, yeah, yeah."

Well, the game starts and the first two times up I hit two ground balls to Joe Gordon. The third time up, it's late in the ball game and the score is tied, 1-1, in the bottom of the eighth. We had two outs and we had our big catcher on first base. Dom [DiMaggio] hit a double. So now first base is open, and Ted is hitting behind me.

Dickey was still catching at the time and he went out to talk to Chandler. They were out there maybe thirty seconds. In the meantime, Ted grabbed me and said, "Listen, Johnny, don't try to pull this guy. What the hell is the matter with you? You got to go up the middle with this guy, or to left field."

I said, "Yeah, yeah, I'll do exactly what you say."

Dickey is on his way back to home plate, and Ted pulls me by the arm and says, "You know damn well they aren't going to walk YOU to get to ME."

I get in the batter's box. Ball one. Strike one. Ball two. Then he threw me that hard sinker away and I just went to left field. Got a base hit. We scored two runs.

Chandler's walking around the mound. He's just chewing my butt out. He says, "You little so-and-so. I'll stick one in your ear next time."

Now, I take a little lead. He's about to pitch to Ted, and he steps off the mound and gives me another blast. Told me what he thought. I told him where he could go. I told him, "Besides, you were a lousy tipper in the Coast League."

Williams hit the first pitch into the triangle for a home run. When he hit it, it sounded like a crack out of a gun.

I score and then I'm in the dugout. No one is saying nothing to me. Now here comes Ted.

A guy says, "Hey, Ted, you really hit that."

He says, "Yeah, that one really felt good. I really got that."

I was sitting next to Bobby and I said, "Geez, I got the big hit this inning and no one said anything to me."

But Ted's looking for me. "Where's that little horn-nosed shortstop of ours?"

Here he comes. He says, "Now, Johnny. Didn't I tell you how to hit Chandler?"

I said, "Let me tell you something, Ted. He was so darned mad at me for getting that dinky little hit, he forgot you were the next hitter."

He laughed like hell and said, "Yeah. You're right!"

For Ted, there were hits in the details. **Bobby Doerr:**

We were at the 1941 All-Star Game. We were in the lobby of the Book-Cadillac Hotel in Detroit. Most of us were together, standing in the lobby. Mr. Hillerich, the founder of the Hillerich Bat Company, was standing there.

Ted went up to him and said, "Mr. Hillerich, I want some 32-ounce bats." I can remember Mr. Hillerich saying, "Ted, you can't get good wood on 32-ounce bats."

Ted said, "What good is wood if you can't handle it?" His theory was, and he proved, if he could have the quickness with a 32-ounce bat to hit the ball with the fat part of the bat, he was much better than having a 34-ounce bat and hitting it on the trademark.

He was always coming up with little things. We had rosin, but it always seemed like our hands were clammy. You didn't get a good grip on the bat. Ted came up with the idea of using olive oil and rosin, which made a sticky substance, which gave you a much firmer grip on the bat.

This also meant that the bat would pick up dirt. It would stick down on the end of the bat. On the prime part of the bat, he had a white spot of about four or five inches. He hit every ball in that area. You could pick up a batting practice bat or a game bat of his, and very, very seldom would you see a white spot anywhere but in that fat part of the bat.

One day, we were in spring training and we were going north. We'd play different towns on our way north. Most every spring, we'd play in Louisville, because they were at that time a farm team for the Red Sox.

The night before, Ted says, "Let's go over to the factory in the morning and watch them turn out bats." We got there about seven-thirty, I think. We had to sit on the steps for about a half-hour until they opened the factory.

We went through looking at some bats. Finally, we ended up with the guy who was back at the lathe, turning out the bats. He was an older man. Ted said to this guy when we got ready to leave, "Anytime you find any little pin knots in wood, put 'em in my bat." They were just little hard spots that would get a little percentage going for you. When Ted left, he handed the guy a twenty-dollar bill. You can bet that Ted got pin knots in his bat.

One time he got an order of bats that didn't feel right to him. When he sent them back, they found out that the handle was just a fraction larger than it should have been. That's how fine he was.

Compulsions, obsessions: **Ted Lyons** *began his twenty-one-year pitching career with the 1923 Chicago White Sox, which meant he pitched plenty to Babe Ruth. Ted knew that. Lyons:*

I got to know Ted fairly well; I pitched against him a lot, and I was in the service with him, out in Hawaii. We rode in a jeep together, every day, in and out of Honolulu. All he'd want to talk about was hitting.

One day, we were riding back from Honolulu, and all of a sudden out of the blue he says to me, "Ted, do you think I'm as good a hitter as Babe Ruth?"

I said, "Well, wait until you get dry behind the ears. You've only been in the league a few years." I was just kidding him.

You know, he wouldn't talk to me all the way home. He just sat there brooding. I had to laugh; I knew what was eating him.

When we got back to the base, I said, "Now, let's get back to the subject. Listen, Ted, you're a little different from Ruth. Babe would hit at balls up around his cap—and those are the ones he'd hit nine miles. You wouldn't swing at one above your letters. Babe didn't mind going after a bad ball. You won't go a half-inch out of the strike zone. You're two completely different hitters." And then I told him, "Of course you're as good a hitter as he was."

Then he was all right again.[1]

*Right-hander **Boo Ferriss** pitched for the Red Sox 1945–50 and then served as a coach:*

When Ted came home from the war, he was anxious to see me. I had won twenty-one games as a rookie. He had heard a lot about it. He was asking questions about me. I was in awe of him, you might say. I was anxious to see him, too. Before the war, I remember going into New York and watching him get 3-for-4 off of Lefty Gomez. Pulled every ball. Shots to right field. Gomez threw bullets. He threw hard.

So my first day of pitching batting practice, he was anxious to hit against me, to get an idea what I was throwing, what my pitches were like. He loved to study pitchers. So he went in the batting cage. Of course, I wasn't bearing down or anything. I was just throwing natural, maybe three-fourths speed.

I guess my ball was moving good. He hit against me and a lot of Boston writers were standing around the cage. Ted came out and asked one of them, "What do you think?" He said, "That kid's going to be all right. He's going to win again. That ball is MOVING."

It was just a thrill to go to the park every day and watch that fellow go to the plate. He was just the greatest swinging that bat. He worked so hard at it, and he studied those pitchers. And he had great concentration. Determination.

He was just beyond everybody on the subject of hitting. I think he was a step ahead of anybody who ever lived and swung a bat. I'm talking about DiMaggio. Mantle. Berra. The top hitters. You didn't see that in any other hitter. He just had that beautiful swing.

Back in those days, the pitchers warmed up right in front of the stands, along the third-base box seats and along the first-base box seats. He'd sit on those steps and look across, and he could see that pitcher warming up and what he was throwing. He'd sit right out there and keep an eye on 'em. He would note something right off, maybe, that was different from what the guy had been throwing. Ted would pick that up. He would mention it. He'd say, "Did you see that? He didn't throw that pitch the last time. He's got something new." Maybe the guy had a slider, or maybe all of a sudden he was throwing sidearm pitches instead of overhand. Ted would tell the other players on the team about it.

He would just catalog those pitches in his mind. Years later, he would just amaze you, talking about Feller and Wynn, Ford and Raschi and those guys. He'd pinpoint what they used to throw against him. All of Ted's attributes weren't physical.

Oh, he had fun. Sometimes during batting practice on an off day or something, he would call out, "Okay, we in Detroit." He loved to hit in Detroit. "We in Detroit. Newhouser is on the mound. The count is two and one. Here he comes . . ." He was just like a kid. He liked to play little games like that. And have fun doing it. Like I always said, he lived for the next time at bat.

He just loved to hit. He might pop up or something, and you'd look out to left field and between pitches, he'd be out there practicing his swing. He was kind of disgusted that the at bat got away from him. I saw him do that. He was just living for the next time at bat. He loved to go to that plate.

He loved to play. He worked so hard at it. If he didn't feel so good one day at the plate, he'd be out the next day working on it. He studied it. He worked hard at it. He'd hit until there was blood running out of his hands.

When I was coaching, I pitched to him a lot. My locker was on the opposite end of the clubhouse from him. I'd be sitting over there at my locker, undressing after a game. He'd come over even before he had showered and he'd push me on the shoulder. "Hey. Nine o'clock in the morning?" The next day, he'd be out there hitting away.

One day at Tiger Stadium, he put on the greatest demonstration in batting practice that I had ever seen. He hit one ball after another, most of them in the upper deck. He loved to hit in Detroit. I think, out of twenty pitches, he hit seventeen up into the stands. And when he got through, it was early, but there were thirty, thirty-five thousand in the stands. Those people just stood and gave him a standing ovation. You would have thought he had just won the World Series.

Ted preached that a large part of hitting was discipline, will, and concentration. He worked obsessively to eliminate distractions. Catcher **Birdie Tebbetts:**

You couldn't distract him. He was intense. Every great hitter was intense. There was only one guy who could shake up Ted Williams, and that was Jake Early. He was a catcher for the Senators. He did a perfect imitation of a tobacco auctioneer, at the time when auctions were popular.

When Williams would get up, Jake Early would auction off a brand of tobacco. Finally, Ted would have to stop the game, call time out, and bust up laughing. He did it about once every series. We all waited for him to do it.[2]

White Sox infielder **Dario Lodigiani:**

Dykes was the manager with the White Sox. Jimmy Dykes was a great bench jockey. So was Mule Haas. We used to get on Ted all the time. Ted had rabbit ears. You'd holler at him, and he'd hear you. He knew you were doing it in a kidding way. And most of the time, it was. He would laugh. He'd get a big bang out of it.

One time, Ted was holding out or something. They wouldn't give him what he wanted, and he made the statement that if he didn't get what he was asking for, he said he was going to be a fireman.

Well, Dykes heard about that. So the first time we played the Red Sox in Chicago, Jimmy Dykes had a siren. You know, the kind that you crank. And he had a fireman's hat on. When Ted Williams walked up there to hit, Jimmy starts in with that siren: *"rrrrrrr-RRRRRRR."* And he's got his fireman's hat on. And Ted Williams backed out and looked in the dugout and he started laughing.

Bobby Doerr:

One day, we were playing a game in Boston. It was a pretty bright day. But a white cloud came by. He's at bat. And I'll always remember, he stepped out of the box when that shadow hit him. Just a few seconds. He let that cloud go by and stepped back in. It was a distraction to him.

Any other ballplayer would have stayed in. That's how sharp he was.

Jack Fadden, *legendary Harvard trainer, also served as trainer for the Red Sox 1950–65:*

Ted does more than study the opposing pitchers. He studies every player, every park. He knows the slant of the batter's box. You've seen him digging at the ground, clawing with his spikes. He knows the height of every pitcher's mound. He knows the throwing power of every outfielder. I found that out one day when he made a hit to right-center.

He ambled down to first, almost to the point of seeming lazy. The next day, with a new club in town, he hit, ran to first, and made the turn at first. It was almost the exact same hit on the very same spot. Why the difference? Ted explained to me about the two outfielders who handled the ball. One was a rockhead; the other was ready and able to throw him out if he didn't hustle. He knows when to conserve energy.

He studies catchers. Certain ones fall into a groove calling pitches. He knows the habits.

He catalogues pitchers. I remember he asked one of the Red Sox kids how a certain pitcher was striking him out. The kid didn't know. Ted said right there and then the kid wouldn't make the big leagues. He didn't. He never found the answer and he never made the big leagues.

Williams doesn't hit just because of what he does that day. It's his advance preparation. He makes sure nothing material hinders him. His sweatshirts have to fit just right.

He breaks in shoes a year in advance. You've seen him tug and twist a cap. That's to make it fit just so. A poor fit might distract him. He'll rip out a worn shoe lacing. Right down to the smallest detail, everything has to be just right. Nothing must interfere. He makes sure of that.

He has an inquisitive mind. If he were at Harvard, he'd be a Phi Beta Kappa.

Sure, he's impulsive, explosive. Complacent people never are great athletes, or great pianists, or great actors, are they?[3]

*Left-hander **Mel Parnell** pitched for the Red Sox 1947–56:*

Everybody said Ted had a God-given talent. He did. No doubt he did. But he worked at it, too. I know cases in Boston when he thought he was seeing too much right-hand pitching, because of the short left-field wall. So when he got on the road and saw left-hand pitching, it made it a little more difficult.

So Maury McDermott and I would pitch batting practice to him, to let him see left-hand pitching. It helped us and it helped him. A lot of times when we pitched batting practice, we wouldn't tell him what was coming. It was up to him to try to figure it out, and it was up to us to try to figure him out. We thought if we could figure him out, the rest of the guys would seem easy.

If Ted were playing today, there's no telling what he'd hit. He'd love to see a young pitcher come in who was just a thrower, not a pitcher. These guys that just rear back and throw the ball. He loved that. His hands would be moving on the handle of the bat so fast, he looked like he was grinding sawdust out of the handle. He couldn't wait.

I remember one day, he was called out on strikes and he came back to the dugout and he was mad as hell. Joe Cronin was our manager at the time. It was 1947. He complained to Cronin that home plate was out of line. All us pitchers, we were sitting on the bench, we just laughed. We thought it was funny. You get called out on strikes, and you think the plate is out of line.

So he and Cronin get into a little heated discussion about it all. So Cronin says, "Let's get the grounds crew out tomorrow and check on it and see if it is out of line."

Well, the next morning about nine o'clock, they got out, they checked home plate, and damned if it wasn't out of line.

I thought Ted was a very underrated outfielder. He was tall and gangly and it didn't look like he had the gracefulness of other outfielders. Of course, playing next to Dominic DiMaggio, who was very graceful, made Ted look a little awkward. But he could make the plays.

On a train traveling, we had a lot of time to discuss baseball. I had a chance to talk to him about hitting. And of course, when he talked about hitting, you just sat and listened. We'd have our dinner and get into little huddles and talk baseball.

He is the only one I've ever heard to determine that there are only three and a half to five inches of good hitting surface on a baseball bat. He made good sense in everything he said about hitting.

He used to talk to the opposition. We used to get after him. Everybody wanted to talk to him about hitting. Everybody around the league, really. We'd get on him. "Hey, don't pass on too much information to those guys. They're the enemy."

I thought Dominic DiMaggio had one of the toughest spots in the lineup, being the leadoff hitter. A lot of times, if

Dom would make out on his first at bat, just as soon as he got back to the dugout, Ted was questioning him. What did that pitcher have? What did he throw? What did he have?

He was always thinking. When he got back from the service, after Korea, he worked real hard to get back into the lineup. He was taking a lot of batting practice. He was getting blisters on his hands. At that time, his agent was Freddie Corcoran. He was a golf pro. Freddie Corcoran suggested that he use a golf glove on his hand to give him a little support and maybe relieve a little of that tenderness.

So Ted started using the golf glove and everybody around the league would see him with a golf glove on. First thing you know, everybody around the league was wearing a golf glove. That's how the batting glove got introduced into baseball. You hear a lot of stories, but that is the original story.

Outfielder **Sam Mele** *broke in with the Red Sox in 1947:*

Ted was in left, Dominic DiMaggio was in center, and I was in right.

I used to warm up with him every day. I'd be on the bench and he'd go out in the field at Fenway and he'd yell, "Okay, Meal. Let's go." He used to call me "Meal." He always wanted me to warm up with him. I was just a friend, I guess.

In '47, in spring training, he used to always want me to sit next to him on the bus rides to exhibition games and talk hitting. That's all he did. He talked about, "Look for this, look for that." The whole thing about hitting. And when you got off the bus, you thought you were the greatest hitter in the world.

In spring training one year, I went to Ted and I talked hitting and hitting and hitting. And then I said, "Well, how about defensive play?" And he said, and this is true, "You go to that little guy in center field." He meant Dom DiMaggio. Ted knew his limitations in the field. And he knew how good Dom was.

Every visiting player that came into Fenway Park used to come out of their dugout to watch him hit. I've seen Mantle, all the big guys, ask him how to hit. And all Ted wanted to talk about was hitting. He'd come out of the cage and talk with these guys.

If he didn't know a pitcher, a guy up from the minor leagues or something, he'd go up and down the bench: "Anybody know this guy? What does he throw? What does he like to throw in a jam? What's his best pitch?" Forever, forever, he wanted every advantage against a pitcher.

Legendary Indiana and Texas Tech basketball coach, and friend to Ted Williams, **Bobby Knight:**

Moose Skowron is a good friend of mine. He told me this story. Moose asked Ted about hitting. Ted said, "You pull the ball too much. You're always trying to hit to left field."

That day, he hit two home runs to right center field at Fenway. When he got in the clubhouse, there was a message on his locker: "Call Ted Williams immediately in the Boston clubhouse."

He calls Ted, and Ted says, "Don't you tell these goddamn Boston writers that I told you to hit the ball to right field."

*Infielder **Jerry Coleman,** who played with the New York Yankees 1949–57:*

It didn't make any difference what team you were on. If you said, "Ted, I'm having trouble hitting the slider," he'd say, "Come over here." He'd spend thirty minutes with you on how to hit the slider.

He probably would have had seven hundred home runs if he hadn't been interrupted in his play by the service. He might literally have been, for power and average, the greatest hitter who ever lived. I would say he was. Period.

*Catcher **Matt Batts** played with the Red Sox 1947–51:*

He just knew everything about hitting, I'll say that. He'd talk to us about it. Not only us, but clubs that would come in, some of the players would ask him to help them with their hitting. He'd have them come out to the park early. He'd help 'em. He wasn't one to not help somebody just because they happened to be on another team.

There was a left-hander with Cleveland. I don't remember who it was. A young phenom left-hander. We went in there, and the sportswriters were saying that this phenom was going to show Williams up. I was sitting out there on the steps watching this pitcher warm up. Ted was there watching him warm up. He turned around to me and said, "He's going to throw me such-and-such a pitch on the third pitch. And I'm going to put it right up in the seats up there."

41

Ted shows off his sweet swing prior to an exhibition game in San Diego in 1940. He is back in his hometown and back in his old home ballpark, Lane Field, where he played with the Pacific Coast League's San Diego Padres. Whenever Ted stepped to the plate, even during batting practice, all eyes were on him.

I guarantee, I think it was the first or second time he was up, he threw him that same pitch and Ted hit it right into that upper deck at that Cleveland Stadium. He was just a genius at those things.

I played against him after I left Boston. He could guess with you. He just was great at knowing what might be thrown to him on a certain pitch. He was just great at knowing when someone might throw him a slider, curve ball, or whatever.

Stealing the signals from second base. He could steal the signal from the catcher about the second time he put the signals down. He could see into the catcher and figure out his change signal. A fastball, he'd have his hands on his knees with them flat on the knee with the fingers pointing down. If it was a curve ball, he'd open his hand and put it across his knee. He was great at catching signals. When I was with the Tigers, I knew if he was on second base, I'd have to be careful.

Mickey Vernon, *who played first base in the big leagues for twenty seasons, mostly with the Washington Senators:*

Playing against Ted? A little scary. Most first basemen, including myself, would play a little deep. We'd move back a few more yards. He hit that sinking line drive that was tough to handle.

He got a lot of base on balls. I never saw him swing at a bad ball, really. His philosophy was, if he started swinging at those balls, a couple of inches off the plate, then the first thing you know the pitcher is going to go a little farther and a little farther. And the next thing you know, the plate is going to be six inches wider than it should be. He was so controlled and so disciplined at the plate that it's hard to judge a present-day player like Ted. He just didn't swing at bad balls.

And when he did, he was not pleased, no matter what the result.
George Sullivan, *the visiting-team batboy at Fenway Park in 1949:*

Some things jump out. Like the home run he hit against Detroit one night. I think it was off Freddie Hutchinson. It was tied and it was getting late. It was around the sixth inning.

In those days, the visiting team clubhouse and the Red Sox clubhouse were right next to one another on the first-base side. It was terrific, because I spent as much time in the Red Sox clubhouse as I did in the visiting team clubhouse. I was always bouncing back between the two clubhouses on errands, before and after the game. Both teams would use the tunnel under the first-base stands.

One of the things you had to cart across the field was a big supply of fresh towels. Hang 'em on the hooks in the dugout. This was a very, very hot night in August. I ran out of fresh towels, because everybody was using them. I had to go back around the sixth inning for towels. I timed it when the Tigers were in the field, and I went across and I waited in the Red Sox dugout until the end of the half inning.

I was just huddled by the stairs there. Anyway, Williams hit one a ton. A typical Williams home run. A mile high. About ten rows into the bleachers, or section one. And there he is galloping around the bases. Nobody galloped around the bases like he did.

He comes across, and they knew enough not to shake his hand at the plate. He didn't like to do that. That used to stir up from time to time crazy stories in the press that he was not speaking to whoever was the on-deck hitter. Well, Ted wouldn't shake hands with anybody up there.

Anyway, here I am seeing Williams hit a titanic home run. I was dying to see his reaction as he came back and down the stairs. Among the first things they were saying to him was, "What kind of pitch was it?"

He was ticked off. He had hit a ball that was not a strike. "I never should have swung at the ball. Lousy pitch."

That hit me as a fifteen-year-old. I loved the guy. But here was a titanic home run that probably was going to win the game. And he was mad about it. At the very least, unhappy about it. It didn't make him a bad guy. But it amazed me. And it bothered me a little bit.

*Others were bothered, too. Excerpts from a piece by syndicated sports columnist **Jim Murray:***

Ted Williams was an objet d'art—and just about as useful. He should be in the Louvre, not Cooperstown. He was probably the greatest pure striker of the baseball that ever lived. But this translated out into exactly one pennant for his team in nineteen years. Only Ty Cobb among the super-hitters has an equally bad in-the-money record.

The object of baseball is victory, not virtuosity. The payoff should be a pennant, not a plaque. Ted Williams' career was a series of nightly and daily batting exhibitions. They had very little to do with baseball, his team or his league.

Ted Williams was on the Red Sox, but not of them, a subtle but real distinction. He gave recitals. The business of winning or losing seemed to belong at a different level. He played the Yankees four times a game. The rest of the team played them nine innings.

Did you ever see Williams field? Did anyone? Steal a key base? Run out from under his hat after a line drive? Crash into a fence? The All-Star Game was his milieu, a show not a struggle. The rest of the year was a one-star game for him.[4]

*Legendary Boston Celtics coach **Red Auerbach,** who was always looking for an edge, remembers running into Ted Williams in the '50s. He found another guy who was always looking for an edge:*

He said to me, "What do you guys eat on the day of a game?"

I said, "What do you want to know for? You seem to be doing all right with what you're doing."

I said, "We have a funny arrangement. On the road, the way it's set up, they get so much per diem and they eat on their own. At home, they eat at home. But the smart ones, for a 7:30 game, will eat around 3:30. You don't want them too full going into a game. I would recommend that."

I said, "What do you do?"

He said, "I have a couple of lamb chops and some tea and toast and I eat after the game." He had the same theory I did. You had to go in hungry. You got to go and play hungry. Like a tiger.

He impressed me so much, because he was a student. A lot of people didn't think of him that way. They thought of him as a flamboyant, happy-go-lucky guy who just went out and played.

He thought of the little things, what's important to being great. When you're great and you excel, some athletes would coast on that. It was very funny. Here's the best hitter in baseball, and he's trying to get another little percentage point.

Red Sox teammate **Eddie Joost:**

He had two lockers. One for him. One for his bats. He'd be over there counting them and feeling them. He'd pick them up and do this and do that. He was always very meticulous with his bats.

George Sullivan, *the former batboy, was a fledgling sports reporter in 1953. He was meeting with Red Sox owner Tom Yawkey when Ted returned from the Korean War in 1953:*

This was a Friday against Detroit. I read in the papers that morning that Ted Williams may show up. Who knows for sure when he'll show up? But he could be at Fenway as early as tonight. Not that he'd play, just that he'd come to the ballpark.

So I show up at the meeting and I'm sitting with Mr. Yawkey in his office and all of a sudden, here he comes, through the door. "Yuh, yuh, yuh," and all of this. So I witnessed Ted coming back from Korea.

I said something about leaving, and Mr. Yawkey said, "No, no, no. Sit down." So I stayed for this meeting. After about twenty minutes, Mr. Yawkey said, "Ted, you're going to hit tonight, aren't you? In batting practice?"

Ted said, "Oh, no. I haven't hit for over a year." He said, "Come on, Ted." Finally he said, "Okay, I'll come down."

So when Ted headed for the locker room, I headed for the batting cage. I wanted to see this.

I was down at the batting cage and here comes Williams. I don't think they had opened the gates yet. But there certainly were a ton of workers around, ushers and concession kids. And the Tigers were starting to play catch in front of their dugout. And here comes Ted. That great stride of his, coming out of the dugout. Everybody starts cheering him, the ushers and the concession kids and everything. And I think probably even the ballplayers.

He gets in the cage. Paul Schreiber was the Red Sox batting practice pitcher. Williams loved him. Everybody loved him. He was a wonderful batting practice pitcher as well as a wonderful human being.

I don't remember what he did with the first couple of pitches, but then he hits one out. He knocked it out of the ballpark. And everybody goes nuts. And the next pitch, he knocks out of the ballpark. Now people are starting to build up. And next pitch comes up. He hits that one out of the ballpark. Now people are yelling. I mean yelling. Schreiber starts to watch the balls go out, to see where they land. He knows they're out. He wants to see how far out.

Now, even though there's only a couple of hundred people, or at the most a couple of thousand people, Williams had to yell at Schreiber to be heard. He's yelling, "Throw the f— ball! Throw the f— ball!" In other words, don't wait and watch. Throw the damn thing. He just wanted to hit the ball. My memory is he hit eight or nine straight out of the ballpark.

People ask me—what was the greatest thing you ever saw Williams do? It was this. He hadn't picked up a bat in fourteen months, or whatever it was. And I don't care if it's Little League. To be able to hit that many balls out.

If you're standing behind the batting cage, with your nose almost pressed up against the net, how far is your nose from the batter's hands—three or four feet? I'm watching and looking. I look and I can see blood coming out from between his fingers. He's hitting the ball and blood is seeping out onto his hands.

Finally he hit the last one out. He just flipped the bat and ran back into the dugout. It was the greatest thing I ever saw him do.

St. Louis Browns first baseman **Chuck Stevens:**

The thing I remember that I saw him do many times is he would walk into the cage and he would begin to hit singles. Bullets. Then he would begin to lengthen out. Just pump a little more effort into the swing. And the last eight or ten or whatever were rattling around up in the seats. He would consistently hit the ball out of sight. The rest of us were standing there with our mouths open. We're grunting to hit one out of there, and he's doing it with ease.

I heard this, and then I later verified it. Ted had an indelible mind, for lack of a better word. Once he saw a pitcher, he knew exactly the series the pitcher used against him and he never forgot it. We were all able to do some of that. I just think Ted NEVER forgot a pitch. The rest of us would let a pitch or two slip our minds. And that was when you went 0-for-4. This indicated to me that this fellow was a once-in-a-lifetime natural. A natural in ways that few people knew about.

Ellis Kinder was a guy who could get Williams out. We had Kinder at the time. Kinder had a plan of his own, because I talked to him about it. Williams would get to the plate and scratch around, making himself comfortable, taking up light housekeeping. Who's going to bother Williams?

The first pitch Kinder would throw to Williams would be right at that back foot, where Williams had dug that hole. Kinder had good luck with him, because Kinder didn't pitch him to any patterned sequence.

If I'm pitching the next day, Ted would go back in the archives of the brain and remember everything that I've done to him. He'd take that to the plate. He was an unusual fellow that way.

Ted would have a guy figured, or it would be a challenge to him until he had him figured. It was a real interesting match. Ted was out there, out-dumbing the pitcher. That's what Ted was doing. Plus, he had eyesight that was unparalleled in baseball. He had a swing that was unparalleled in baseball. Plus, he was working at it every moment of his life.

You could see that when he was in the batting cage. You take a lot of guys who are taking batting practice, and for them it's kind of laughing-and-scratching time. Not with Williams. No one ever suggested that he leave that cage early. That was his domain. He was absolutely locked into what he was doing at the plate. No jazzing around. He was taking care of business.

You take all these factors, and you've got a guy who's whacking that baseball at a .400 clip.

We're playing in Boston. I can't remember if it was a close ball game—with the Browns, there weren't too many close ones. I'm playing deep. Williams is at the plate. The base is open. He hit a shot between me and the foul line. I dove at the ball. Got my glove on the ball. It took the glove off of my hand. I reached and got the ball and threw him out at first base.

Playing first base, if he hit one between you and the second baseman, all you would see was a little puff of dirt. And I'm thinking, *Hoo-boy. I'm glad I wasn't in front of THAT thing.*

We're playing Boston in St. Louis. It's late in the season, which means the field is as hard as the floor you're standing on, because both ball clubs (Cardinals and Browns) were using the diamond and it's hotter than Hades in St. Louis.

Ted hit a ball. I jump for it. I didn't get it. I swear the ball, with such topspin, went down behind me and bounced fifty feet in the air. We were lucky to hold him to a single.

I go over now to hold him on. He's out there moaning. "Geez, I should have hit that ball out of the park. I hit the upper half of it." I called time and said, "What are you talking about, you hit the upper half of it?" He says, "Yeah, I hit the ball on the upper half."

Ted retired after the 1960 season, but he never stopped studying the science of hitting. The famous legend coached Red Sox hitters during preseason training, and his booming arrival in camp became a rite of spring. Young, impressionable players never forgot a critique from the Splendid Splinter. When Ted's successor in left field, Carl Yastrzemski, struggled at the plate, Williams was summoned from his favorite fishing hole. Pitcher **Charlie Wagner,** *who went on to serve in the team's front office:*

I remember when Yaz first came up. Yaz was hitting like hell down in the minors. He wasn't hitting when he came to the big leagues. You know, Yaz used to have his bat up high when he hit. Ted said, "Yaz, you know, one of these days, you're going to definitely have to come down with that bat. Now that you're young, you're able to shoot it from there. As you get older, you're going to have to bring the bat down." And by God, as Yaz got older, he brought the bat down.

*Red Sox first baseman **George Scott** played for the Red Sox 1966–71, 1977–79. He was among the generations of Boston farmhands tutored by visiting legend Ted in spring training:*

I had just signed with the Red Sox. I can remember Ted coming by in the spring, over to Ocala, Florida. For some reason, he used to get at me a lot. You know: "Awwww, you think you can hit. Awww, you can't hit."

I remember this specific day during one of our spring games, I hit a ball off the top of the center-field fence in Ocala. That ball must have went about 450 feet. And when I came into the dugout, he was saying, "Awwwww, you should have hit it out!"

Ted taught all of the young people who came through the Red Sox organization an awful lot. There were a lot of things that I carried through my entire career that I learned from Ted Williams.

We were all young fellows at the time—eighteen, seventeen years old. When we looked up the road, when he came up that hill, you could hear him coming. He'd be talking as he's coming. Then he'd get near me and he'd say, "GEORGE Scott. GEORGE Scott, my ass." I was one of the guys he liked, because he liked my work ethics: first player to get there, last player to leave. I think Ted Williams appreciated that in a player.

And I listened to him. There were a lot of number-one draft choices, and guys like that he was a little tougher on because they didn't listen to him. Everybody respected him. Everybody was happy to have him around. When he came around, you knew it was going to be a helluva day.

I remember him getting into the batting cage one day. [Tony] Conigliaro and myself, we were all hanging around the batting cage. And he got in there with his street clothes on. He said, "Let me show you guys how to hit."

And he got in there and he called, "Line drive to center field." He hit a line drive to center. He said, "A line drive to right." He hit a line drive to right. He said, "Line drive to left." He hit a line drive to left. And at that time, he had to be in his fifties. And you could see why he was such a great hitter.

When he was managing over in Washington, I'd go and talk to him all the time. Because I knew that he had a lot of good ideas about hitting. I never thought that I could be Ted Williams. I always thought that you had to have outstanding hand-eye coordination where you did not swing at bad balls. You had to be very patient. I was not that kind of a patient hitter. But the other parts, about getting that bat through the hitting zone and being quick with the bat—these were things I tried to learn from. As far as being patient and taking walks, as much as he took walks, I wasn't that patient.

*Record producer **Ed Penney,** who handled young Red Sox star Tony Conigliaro's singing career in the 1960s, visited the Ted Williams Baseball Camp in Lakeville, Minnesota, in the summer of 1967:*

Both of my boys went to Ted's baseball camp that year—Wayne and Chip. They were there for the summer term. They loved it down there. They particularly were impressed by the fact that Ted was there. He didn't just lend his name to it. Ted did show up and worked with them. He obviously enjoyed children.

My wife and I went down there on the final day, which would have been the day before Tony got hit. Ted invited us into his cabin, which was his office. He invited us to stop in for a few minutes. We talked about the Red Sox, and at the time he said he had been watching them, all the games on television. He said, "You've got to realize that it's a distinct possibility that they could go all the way. They could win the pennant."

He then told me that he felt that Tony was standing too close to the plate. He said, "When it's this tight, they're going to start throwing at him. And he's got to be alert. But he's up too close to the plate."

We talked for probably an hour. Just chatting about baseball in general, about the Red Sox. He had strong opinions about the Red Sox and the rest of the American League. It was obvious that he kept up with it like an avid fan would.

The last thing he said to me as he was walking away, he turned to me and said, "Now don't forget to tell Tony what I told you. Don't forget." It was like he was thinking of it as he walked away, and he wanted to emphasize it.

The next night, I went to the clubhouse and told Tony what Ted had said. Tony just laughed. He was in a batting slump. He said, "Who would want to hit me now?" Of course, he was hit that night.

Ted finally agreed to put his big mouth and expertise on the line when he signed up to manage the Washington Senators in 1969. And he found another young group to lecture on the science of hitting: pitchers. Senators right-hander **Dick Bosman:**

The lessons I learned from Ted Williams are all very positive, in spite of the fact that he hated pitchers. He told us that.

Casey Cox was pitching one day in the old Kansas City ballpark. It was our first year with Ted, in '69. Casey was pitching a pretty good ball game, but he was walking a few people here and there. We had the lead, but it was getting away from us, because Casey wasn't pitching as well as he should have.

I was sitting down by the water cooler there, trying to mind my own business. Ted came down and drop-kicked the water cooler and scared the hell out of me. He looked at me and said, "You know, Bosy, when I played, I hated pitchers. And I'm having a hard time liking you guys."

As a real competitive guy and as the real fierce, competitive hitter that he was, that was his feeling about pitchers.

But, on the other side of it, very early in the spring of 1969, he said to me, "You know, you got a chance to be pretty good." You know, he had that sarcastic way about him. A lot of it was tongue-in-cheek, but a lot of it was that truth-spoken-in-jest thing. Looking at my history at that point, it wasn't much. I was just a young guy struggling. The year before wasn't a very good year. We were bad, but I was bad, too.

So he said to me, "You've got a chance to be pretty good, but you've got to learn to use what you've got." I said, "Well, when do we start?" He said, "We already have."

From then on, it was more a learning process for me, through him, to learn how to set up hitters. How to pitch properly with what I had. The cat-and-mouse game that we all enjoy so much as pitchers, and hitters, too. There's no question it was a turning point in my career. From 2-9 to 14-5 and the ERA title. The next year, 16 wins. I didn't add a pitch to my repertoire. It was a matter of learning to use what I had.

He taught me how to set up hitters. What's a hitter looking for in this count? This is what you've got to pitch to him. You've got to learn to turn that around a little bit. If a hitter is looking for this, you're going to have to throw him that. And once he starts looking for this, no-o-o-w this pitch becomes a little more effective for you.

As a hitter, he basically studied pitchers' tendencies, their abilities and what they went to in different situations. He was a bright guy. That's a common trait among all great athletes. They can remember things when they're needed the most. Ted, with his abilities, couple that with the fact that he damn near knew what was coming all the time.

He was a big believer in the slider. He felt like the slider was a damn tough pitch to hit. I had a pretty good one. He taught me how to use that slider to set up my fastball. And to learn how to go back and forth between pitches. He was a big believer, with two strikes, to show them something different. Show them a different delivery. I was able to throw a little sidearm along with my overhand stuff. Those things were the bottom line. Much of what I use today as a coach is because of what I learned from Ted.

I think he would tell you this, too. He never made much of a study of managing, because he was so tied up in what he did best, which was hitting.

*First baseman **Don Mincher,** a veteran big leaguer who was traded to Washington in 1969:*

The first words I spoke to him when I joined the club in Chicago when I was traded there: I walked out on the field and told him who I was. He said, "Yeah, I want to talk to you about your stroke." It wasn't, "Hello, how are you? How's your family? Good to see you." It was, "I want to talk to you about your stroke." Well. I was really excited about that. But it was the first time I was ever greeted that way by someone I'd never met in my life.

We talked. And he was right on. I was maybe a little bit above a mediocre career, maybe on the tail end of my career. But he was interested in every hitter in the American League—I promise you he could tell you something about everybody, not only on our club, but every other club.

We were not very good. But there was not a lot of instruction in the Ted Williams regimen as far as playing winning, fundamental baseball. The thing he was proudest of, the thing he really tried, was the offensive part of the game. That's what he really emphasized. I think that's the way it was about a lot of aspects of his life. He had a passion about some things. And he lived it to the fullest. But fundamental baseball was not one of them.

Where he was really forceful was when you had an at bat and it was really crummy. He would immediately, when you came back to the bench, be very forceful about what you did wrong, what you should have done. That's the only time I ever saw him really, really forceful. Almost to the point of upset.

Here's a guy who hit .340 all of his life. He just could not understand why an average player could not hit AT LEAST .300 and drive in eighty and hit twenty home runs. That was just a concept that he did not, or could not, understand. He could not understand why anyone could not do that. The game's a little tougher for some of us. His impatience showed over our lack of executing the things he was trying to teach us.

Ted always believed in the theory that you hit with a little upswing. Your swing has to have a little upward motion about it. He noticed that my swing was somewhat more of a downswing—which a lot of teachers were teaching at that time. Hit down on the ball. That Charlie Lau stuff. Ted was just the opposite. Hands close to the body. Short stride. Swing a little up. I was there ten minutes and I was in the cage, working on that stuff. Because Ted Williams said them.

I've seen him explode and cuss and raise Cain more times when a hitter swung at the first pitch he saw in a ball game and made an out with it. Popped it up. He would go ballistic. He always believed, if you swing at the first pitch, now you've seen a fastball or a curve ball that you made an out on, and you still haven't seen the pitcher's repertoire. He believed in taking the first pitch, always. Unless it was late in the ball game, same pitcher pitching, and you had seen him four times.

A lot of hitters go up there with the theory that you swing at the first good thing you see, because you may not get it again. Well, Ted completely discounted that theory. You walk up there in the first inning and you swing at the first thing you see and pop it up, he would explode.

Of course, that's old-school baseball. I saw him just get turned inside out and go crazy when hitters swing at the first pitch and make an out. I think that was the biggest thing that he tried to teach.

He didn't ever, that I remember, emphasize hitting behind the runner, advance the runner, changing your thinking with a man on third and fewer than two outs. The theory always was the same. Right or wrong, that was his theory. It was never to manufacture a run—a walk, a bunt, and a single, or a double; hit behind him to move him to third, score on a fly.

He never thought that way. Your hitting should be the same every time.

The pitchers loved him. Everybody liked him. I mean, the personality of Ted Williams is one that I have never seen met. I mean, he could just really sell you on an idea quickly. He just had that kind of personality.

Pitchers had a lot of respect for him because he had studied pitching so much—from the hitting aspect. He knew how he was going to be pitched from every pitcher he ever faced. He would talk to the pitcher about that. The pitch sequence. Pitching inside-outside. And the pitchers really did learn a lot from him.

I would say this—the pitchers had much more respect from him as far as learning than some of the hitters did. Because hitters are hardheaded. They're going to do things their way. And if it wasn't Ted Williams's way, it was the wrong way. That's where the impatience came in. If you were a pitcher and you went out there and got creamed, he talked civil.

No matter what anyone else says, he really did want to win. I think there were just some things lacking on our ball club. It came to a point where it just was, "What else could I do?"

He might have rubbed some guys the wrong way. He didn't rub me the wrong way. I could say that it was a joy to play for him. But somewhat it was not a good thing that he was a manager in the first place. I think his life involved hitting. Period. And if you'll notice, most of the successful managers are players that were very mediocre players. I think of Billy Martin, Dick Williams. Go right on down the line. They had to scrap and learn how to win. For Ted Williams, it was easy to do the thing he loved. And that was hit.

It was frustrating to see us lose and lose and lose. I think given the right makeup of a ball club, I think Ted probably would have been successful. I don't know. We didn't have a very good fundamental club. Didn't teach it in spring training. For those things, that's where his lack of managerial ability showed. Everything else, he was terrific. I wouldn't take anything for my years with him. I learned a lot. And I got to be with my hero for a little while. My lasting vision of him is sitting on the bench and talking hitting on and on and on.

Old habits never die and never fade away. Prior to the 1982 season, sixty-three-year-old Ted agreed to play in the first ever Red Sox Old Timers Day that summer. **George Sullivan,** *who was then the Red Sox public relations director:*

It was during spring training, and the team was playing out of town somewhere. It was about two o'clock in the afternoon, and I was in my office and it was very quiet.

All of a sudden, I hear the ball hitting a bat. CRACK. CRACK. CRACK. I said, "I wonder who stayed behind?"

This was coming from the main diamond. I was curious, so I went out and who was it but Ted, taking batting practice.

I came behind the cage and I said, "You don't care about this Old Timers game, huh?" That's what he was doing it for.

Past his eightieth birthday and into the twenty-first century, Ted Williams, the man who talked hitting with Babe Ruth, Rogers Hornsby, Ty Cobb, and anybody who wandered into earshot,

talked hitting with teenage batsmen. Former Red Sox teammate **Boo Ferriss,** *who was the long-time baseball coach at Delta State University in Mississippi, remembers a trip to the Ted Williams Museum and Hitters Hall of Fame in Hernando, Florida:*

My college team that I coached for twenty-six years, in '99, they had a tournament in Lakeland, Florida. I was retired. But I called Ted up and told him, "Our team is coming down to play in Lakeland. It's right on the way to the museum. Will you speak to them?"

He said, "Bring 'em on. Bring 'em on."

So we stopped over there and for thirty minutes, he had them spellbound. He had them pop-eyed.

They wheeled him in in a wheelchair, and before I could say anything, Ted was saying, "Give me a bat! Give me a bat!"

Former Delta State player **Dee Haynes,** *currently in the St. Louis Cardinals minor-league system:*

We had a great time at the museum. And then we knew the second that Ted Williams came in the door. Even though he had had a stroke and he was in a wheelchair, and he doesn't see real good, the man is just fiery. He had a real loud, carrying voice that demands attention.

We went into a little room there. Just had some bleachers around the side. A little stage-type deal. He got up there and talked hitting. That's what he does. He said, "Somebody go get me a bat." One of the workers went and tracked down a bat.

He got some volunteers to go up there, and he showed them some techniques he believed in. You can't really say the man is wrong. The best hitter in the game in what, seventy years?

I was lucky enough to be one of the volunteers. I went up there, face-to-face with him. To see this man you read books about and everything. Being a great baseball fan, I had read several biographies and such. It was almost like I couldn't really understand what he was saying, because I was just thinking how cool it was. To actually have him touch your hands and place them where he would on a bat. It was only for a few minutes, but it was cooler than anything you can really imagine.

TEDDY BALLGAME

*When he walked into the batter's box and looked out at that
pitcher, it was with utter disdain.*
—ST. LOUIS BROWNS FIRST BASEMAN CHUCK STEVENS

Disdain, joy, ambivalence, anger, petulance, pettiness, play-
fulness. On the baseball field, Ted Williams could do it all.

Some of the famous greats of the game, such as Joe DiMaggio, were strictly business. They played the game stone-faced
and stoic and regal. No one ever knew the great DiMaggio's
true emotions.

Ted was the straightforward type. The only mystery was
which true emotion would come frothing forth next.

Teddy Ballgame appeared to take it all personally, and it
showed. While DiMaggio glided, Ted galloped, swaggered,
pouted, laughed, twisted, flapped, fidgeted, loafed, swore,
heaved bats, and grumbled. Stoic? In high school, he would
watch ball four and burst into tears. Of course it was personal.
Pitchers weren't walking him; they were taking away his
chance to hit.

Ted enjoyed the intensity and tension of a good joust and a spirited duel, and they were everywhere on the baseball field. Pitchers weren't trying to get him out; they were trying to embarrass him. Faraway fences were taunting him to try to hit a ball to the other side. Just go ahead and try.

The fans taunted him, and he taunted back. Why shouldn't he? The newspapermen taunted him on the newsstand every morning and night, and he showed how he felt about them, sometimes right in the middle of an inning.

It was part of his game. Ted was fascinated and motivated by difficulty. He tinkered with knuckle balls, because he had a hard time hitting them. He loved to square off with Bob Feller, because it was most fun to beat the best. He wanted to bat .400, because nobody had done it for a while. It looked pretty hard. He adored challenges and turned them into dares.

It was a dare when opposing teams, most notably Lou Boudreau's Cleveland Indians, shifted their defenses way over to the right. Ted refused to give in and accept free, dinky singles to left, one after the other. Of course he wouldn't give in. He simply smashed hits straight into the shift.

No intelligent pitcher would brush him back, knock him down, or buzz him close. That kind of thing was only daring Ted Williams to strike back.

Big occasions were a chance to show them all on big stages: All-Star Games, the World Series, the last at bat of his career. And if there was nothing to shoot for, say on a humdrum day on the practice field, he concocted challenges—throwing contests, long-ball bets. It kept life interesting, and fun, and challenging. Otherwise, baseball would be just another business.

Oakland Oaks infielder **Dario Lodigiani:**

At San Francisco, at Seals Stadium, was probably one of the nicest minor-league ballparks in the country. To hit a ball over that right-field fence was 350-something feet. Down the lines.

Ted Williams, he came in one day and they asked him about it. He said, "Before the year is over, I'm going to hit one over that thing."

Damned if he didn't.

Red Sox teammate **Eldon Auker:**

One time we were in St. Louis—in 1939. Buck Newsome was pitching for St. Louis. He was a pretty good pitcher. The first time Ted was up, he struck out. First time he ever saw Newsome.

He was coming back to the bench, and Newsome was standing out on the pitcher's mound with his glove up to his face and he was laughing at Ted. We said, "Look, Ted, Newsome's laughing at you."

Ted said, "He's WHAT?" We said, "He's laughing at you. He struck you out." Well, geez, Ted went into a tirade.

Next time up, Ted hit a home run. As he went around the bases, he said, "Laugh that one off!"

Next time up, he hit another home run. Ted ran around the bases saying, "Now have a good laugh. Go ahead and laugh, you so-and-so."

He rode him all the way around the bases. I don't think Newsome ever laughed at him again.

My roommate was Tommy Bridges when I was with Detroit. They traded me to Boston in 1939 for Pinky Higgins.

The first time we went into Detroit to open up the '39 season, I had dinner with Tommy Bridges, my old roommate, the night before the game. We were very close friends. He said, "What about this guy Williams they're talking about? Is he the kind of ballplayer the newspapers are talking about?"

I said, "He's pretty good. I'll bet you before we get out of here, he'll hit one out of here over those right-field stands." They had just put in new stands in right field, a double-decker. I said, "Before we get out of here, he'll hit one out of here."

Tommy said, "Well, I'll have to see that. I don't think anybody is going to hit one out of here."

I think it was either the first or second time up, Ted hit one over the stands. Tommy was over in the other dugout. He waved at me and shook his head at me.

Ted did exactly what I said he would do. I knew he would.

Red Sox teammate **Sam Mele:**

One day, we're playing Detroit. The wind is blowing in terribly from right field. He always came out to look at the flag. And he said, "Geez, there'll be no home runs hit to right field today."

Well, he hit a ball to right field and it cut right through the wind. Home run.

Red Sox pitcher **Mel Parnell:**

One day, Pedro Ramos struck out Ted Williams. After the game, he came into the clubhouse with the ball that he struck Ted Williams out with and wanted it autographed.

Ted told him, "I don't sign any ball I struck out on." He was giving him a little bit of a rough time, you know? Teasing him, more or less.

After a while, you could see tears coming to Pedro's eyes. Because he wanted that ball signed, by all means. After teasing him for a while, Ted says, "Give me the ball. I'll sign that damn thing." So he signed the ball and gave it to him. Pedro went out of the clubhouse with a smile on his face, happy as a lark. He had the ball signed by Ted Williams that he struck him out with.

The next time Pedro pitches to Ted, he hits one halfway up the right-field bleachers. Ted hollers, "You find that SOB, and I'll sign it, too!"

He was that way about everything. I remember one time we had a driving match with golf balls. Against Babe Zaharias. This was in Sarasota. She was a great pro golfer. And Ted was dead serious about this. You'd think he'd just go out there and try to hit the ball. But he took it very serious. He was very determined. He wanted to beat her; it wasn't just a game with him.

I remember one day, he had a throwing contest with Billy Goodman. Billy didn't have the strongest arm in baseball. They were doing this in Washington, D.C.

They were throwing to the bullpen. Ted threw, and I think his ball hit the wall of the bullpen. Billy's ball went into the bullpen, and Billy Goodman beat him. That almost killed him.

Ted was upset about it and was kidding Billy. Told him he had a bologna arm. He was always having fun. He enjoyed the game. He had a lot of little boy in him.

Tommy Henrich *played outfield for the New York Yankees:*

I remember the year Williams came up, 1939. Early in the season, he and I were sitting in Yankee Stadium talking about hitting the long ball. He'd already hit some clouts, one out of Briggs Stadium, one out of here, one out of there.

"Did anyone ever hit a ball out of Yankee Stadium?" he asked.

"No," I said, "and don't get any dumb ideas, either."

"Why?"

"It's farther than you think."

He looked out toward right field. Sort of measuring it. I just knew what he was thinking.

So the next time they came to New York, I was watching them taking batting practice. Ted caught ahold of one. It was a beauty. Man, he drilled that thing up into the third deck, right into an exit. Quite a shot. But still not out. I yelled, "Hey, Ted." He turned around. "You give up?" I asked. He grinned and yelled back, "Hey, don't tell anybody I said that, huh?" But he had ideas about doing it.[1]

*Red Sox teammate **Eddie Joost**:*

One night against Washington, we were playing against a left-handed pitcher. Early in the game, Ted popped the ball up with two men on and two out. He pointed to the pitcher and said, "I'll get it right. Don't worry about it."

Ted trades hats with Red Sox coach and baseball funnyman Al Schacht. On the baseball field, Ted displayed the total range of emotions.

AUTHOR'S COLLECTION

As so often happens with those guys, later in the game, he hit a home run into the bleachers. And he bounced all the way around the bases. He was saying, "I told you! I told you!"

St. Louis Browns first baseman **Chuck Stevens:**

When he walked into the batter's box and looked out at that pitcher, it was with utter disdain.

At the plate, it was war. It was absolutely declared war with him. He carried it to the ultimate. He knew who he was. That's the important thing. There was no doubt in his mind that he was the best. And almost every day, he'd show you.

Red Sox teammate **Bobby Doerr:**

On the way north in 1939, we were playing in Atlanta. A pop fly, I think it was in foul territory.

He went over and he dropped the ball. He picked the ball up and threw it over the stands.

Chuck Stevens:

One time we were in Boston and Ted's PO'ed at the writers—he got that way about once a week. We were on the bench and somebody says, "Did you see Williams?"

I look up and he's got his feet crossed out there in left field. His glove is hanging by his wrist. There's a ball game going on!

White Sox and Athletics infielder **Dario Lodigiani:**

In Fenway Park, down the left-field line, the people were so close to the left-fielder. The way the stands were, the fans were looking straight down at Ted Williams. They used to heat up pennies and quarters and they'd throw them out to him, and Ted would go pick 'em up and he'd drop them. I saw that a lot of times.

The dugout was down left field, and you could hear him hollering at those fans up there, "You New England sons of bitches!" We were right there. They used to get on him. Finally, they put some security out there. Anybody got on Ted, they'd run them out of there.

Boston Braves outfielder **Max West:**

One time, I was hit in the mouth during a game. I was taking a drink of water. The water fountain was next to home plate. Paul Waner was hitting, and he was notorious for hitting foul balls on the third-base side. I was just about to take a drink, and he fouled a ball off and hit me right in the mouth.

So I had to stay home from the next road trip. My lips looked like liver. So my wife and I went out to see the Red Sox play. We sat over on the third-base side. And old Ted, somebody got on him. There was this big, big guy. I think he went to both ballparks. He was big enough to take up two seats. He was yelling at Ted. You know how close the seats were.

In the fifth or sixth inning, Ted came in, right about where we were sitting. And he pointed at this guy. He said, "You. YOU. You up there. Yeah, you know who I'm pointing at. You're a SON OF A BITCH." He just yelled it out.

My wife said, "What goes with this guy?" I said, "Oh, he's all right. He doesn't mean anything. He's just a big kid. And having a ball."

Joe Heving, *who pitched for the St. Paul Saints against the Minneapolis Millers and young Ted Williams:*

We were a run behind in the eighth inning. We had runners on first and second with two out. The batter hit a ball to right. Williams should have caught it. He got a slow start. The ball hit his glove on the first bounce. It hurt his hand. So instead of chasing the ball, he stood there shaking his fingers.[2]

Former Red Sox first baseman **Mickey Vernon:**

I was on deck. He was nearing his four-hundredth home run. Earlier in the game, the fans in left field were getting on him a little bit. I forget what the reason was.

Ted never bothered to shake your hand if you hit a home run. He'd wait until you got in the dugout and hit you on the leg or something. And if he hit a home run, he didn't expect you to stick out your hand and shake hands with him. If you did, he would just slap it and keep on running into the dugout.

This particular time I was thinking, *Geez, I've got to shake hands with him. It's his four-hundredth home run.* So I stuck out my hand, and he spits at the press, at the fans, and everybody else. I never did get to shake his hand. I stuck it out there, but he was spitting.

Joe Cronin, *Red Sox manager 1935–47, then general manager, on Ted's spitting:*

It's no secret. We, the Red Sox, were distressed. We couldn't condone it. We fined him and he said it would never happen again.

But don't those things happen in baseball? After all, the guy's living in a fishbowl. The nerves get ruffled. Yours would, too.

I remember a day in Philadelphia when I was playing and nothing was going right. The fans used to sit up in the second deck, hanging over the dugout. They'd fill paper bags with orange peels and every time I'd go to the bench, I'd get showered.

This particular day, I just couldn't take it any longer. They were on me and I burned. I went to the ice bucket and grabbed every cube I could hold. I stood on the dugout steps and kept throwing ice cubes at them, as fast as I could fill my fists.

I was mad. I was throwing ice cubes in a fury. But to this day, I'll never be able to explain why. I don't know what happened to me, and no matter how much I think about it, I get no closer to an explanation.

Didn't Joe Kuhel once take a poke at a writer in Washington? Kuhel was quiet, always a gentleman. But he exploded. I read somewhere that Bob Meusel of the Yankees did the same thing.

The players involved probably have all felt as I did later. They probably all asked themselves: Why? I couldn't tell you.

Neither could Ted tell me.[3]

On September 21, 1958, Ted took a called third strike and heaved his bat in anger. The bat bounded into the stands and conked Gladys Heffernan on the head. She was the sixty-year-old housekeeper of Red Sox general manager Joe Cronin and a big Ted Williams fan. **Maureen Cronin,** *daughter of Joe Cronin:*

I wasn't at the ballpark; I was at school. When I came home, my mother was in the kitchen, and she was very upset. She said, "Gladys has been hit in the head with a bat by Ted Williams."

I said, "Oh, Mother. Gladys is only four feet eleven inches, and she's this little tiny Englishwoman, and she couldn't possibly be hit over the head by a bat by Ted Williams." It turns out that's exactly what happened.

Ted went to see her in the hospital every single day and bought her a beautiful diamond wristwatch. I think he felt worse about it than anybody.

Dad moved our box seat back three boxes so we weren't right on the field anymore.

Boyishness didn't always mean throwing tantrums. Ted liked fun, too. **Johnny Sain,** *who pitched for the Yankees and Boston Braves, was Williams's classmate during preflight training in World War II:*

We'd play ball on the weekends when we had the time. This was in Chapel Hill. I'd throw a lot of batting practice. There was a long right field at this ballpark. It was very deep.

One day, he hit a ball out of the ballpark off of me. He said I'd bet him Cokes for the crowd that he couldn't do it.

I don't remember betting him. But we went into the clubhouse, and I had to buy Cokes for the ball club.

Athletics infielder **Eddie Joost:**

I was playing shortstop, and he would almost never hit anything to the left side of the infield. He defied everybody and would never bunt, of course. They pulled a shift on him. We pulled a shift on him, but not as drastic as Boudreau's.

I was with the Athletics. Ted was on second base. The ball was kind of hit high over the pitcher's mound between the pitcher and third base. I came flying in there to pick the ball up and reached down to catch it and all of a sudden the ball disappeared.

I couldn't understand where the ball went. I looked in my glove. It wasn't there.

What I discovered later: The ball hit the heel of my glove. In those days, we had those big, heavy old shirts with the big sleeves. The son of a gun went up the left arm of my sleeve and ended up in back of me, inside my shirt.

So Williams is looking at me and he's starting to move toward third base. He started to go, and then he jumped back, and he started to go again.

I said, "If you run, I'll tackle you. I don't know where the ball is, but I'll tackle you. You're not gonna go."

He goes back to second, laughing like hell.

Red Sox first baseman **George Scott:**

He would hit me ground balls in spring training. We would get in a betting game. Like he would say, "If you catch fifty in a row, I owe you a Cadillac." Every time I see him, I ask him for my Cadillac. I won quite a few Cadillacs from him.

He was competitive and he'd make you competitive. He'd go to hit a ground ball and he'd say, "You catch this one, you

Ted keeps his head in and crushes a pitch. In the batter's box, his concentration was complete. He once called time-out to allow a cloud to pass overhead.

NATIONAL BASEBALL HALL OF FAME

got a Cadillac!" He'd rip it to my right, hard with topspin, and I'd get it and he'd say, "Ohh, foootz. You got a Cadillac."

History often dared him. When Giants first baseman Bill Terry hit .401 in 1930, twelve-year-old Ted decided he wanted to grow up to do that. Going into the final day of the 1941 season—a double-header against the Athletics in Philadelphia—Ted's average was .39955. It was clearly time to rise to the occasion. Williams went 6-for-8 in the two games to finish at .406, the last .400 season in the big leagues. Red Sox manager **Joe Cronin:**

In Washington, Sid Hudson held him to a double in three trips and his average dropped a point to .405. The next day,

Dutch Leonard and Dick Mulligan stopped him with just a single in seven trips and we moved into Philadelphia for the final three games of the season.

Ted asked coach Tom Daly if he'd pitch to him on the open date, Friday. Imagine that. The guy at .401 and he wanted to work. His timing was off, he said. So I told Daly to get two dozen new baseballs that would spring off his bat. Get that confidence up.

Connie Mack had told the Athletic pitchers publicly they were not to walk Ted. They were to make him get his hits, or fall.

He got four hits in the opener to get to .404. There was never a question about taking him out of the lineup. He didn't want it. I never gave it a thought. The stories that I offered to take him out and he refused were just bits of imagination. I put him in there automatically. He played as always in the second game.

The A's pitched a new kid, Fred Caligiuri, who held the Sox to six hits—two of them by Ted and one of them a shot that went through a loudspeaker in right field, as clean as a bullet.[4]

Red Sox teammate **Charlie Wagner:**

You can't believe what he had to do to get to .400. That's a large number. The thing is, hitters like Hornsby and Cobb, they could run. Ted was not slow, but he wasn't any speedster. He wasn't slow-slow, but he couldn't make any infield hits. Ted had to get clean base hits.

You can't believe how many hits he had to get. And it was an everyday thing. He had to get base hits. And he accomplished that in good fashion. He'd win a ball game for you. He won a lot of ball games doing his thing.

Every day, he'd come to the room and say, "Geez, I felt good today."

Dares and challenges were everywhere. Cleveland player-manager Lou Boudreau made the Williams Shift famous in 1946, but several teams had dreamed up variations. Infielder **Dario Lodigiani:**

We used a shift against him when I was with the White Sox. There was no third baseman. The third baseman would play shortstop. The shortstop would play on the other side of second base. The second baseman would play where the first baseman would usually play. The first baseman would play down the line.

Ted was a hardhead, in a way. They knew that we were defensing him that way, but he was determined to drive a ball through there anyway.

I remember in Boston, we put the switch on him. He'd pop a ball to left field, and he'd laugh like heck running down the base line. Nobody was there, and the ball would fall in.

Indians infielder **Ray Boone:**

I was playing short, and I'd go over and play second. The third baseman would come over and be behind the bag.

One day, Ted laid a bunt down the third-base line. He did it because people were always ranting and raving, "Why didn't he bunt?" We were glad when he bunted, because we knew where he was at—he was at first base; he wasn't rounding the bags on a home run.

The fans went wild. I ran over and got the ball, and you could hear him over at first base, ranting and raving. He didn't want to do that.

I couldn't hear what he was saying, but I could hear him growling over at first base.

Red Sox teammate **Charlie Wagner:**

I remember sitting with Ted and Ty Cobb one time. Cobb wanted Ted to hit to left when they put the shift on, the Boudreau Shift, when everybody was on the right side of the diamond.

Cobb was trying to explain to him, "Go to left field. Go to left field."

And Ted says, "That's what they WANT me to do. Besides, they can't play me high enough, because if I'm hitting right, I can hit 'em out of the park."

Cobb says, "Yeah, but you can get a lot of hits to left field."

Ted said, "They want me to hit singles. They don't want me to hit home runs."

Ted used to hit them between them on the right side, anyway. He used to hit them hard enough.

On September 13, 1946, the Red Sox clinched the American League pennant with a 1-0 victory over Cleveland. The run came on a Ted Williams home run. An inside-the-park home run, to left field, against the Boudreau Shift. Red Sox pitcher **Boo Ferriss:**

I can see him right now. Those long legs going.

We were in old League Park. Right field wasn't 270 or 250 feet. You'd have to get the ball in the air somewhat, but it wasn't anything to hit home runs in that park.

The third baseman was over toward shortstop. They had the shift on. The Boudreau Shift. Ted hit the ball right over what would have been the third baseman's head, if they had been playing normal. Just inside the left-field line. Left field was fairly deep.

The ball rolled all the way to the wall. The left-fielder was playing way over in center field. Ted made it all the way around those bases. It was something to see.

We were all up on the top of the dugout, hollering, "Come on, Ted. Come on, Ted." We didn't know whether he was going to make it or not. He wasn't used to running that far.

He made it. He slid into home plate. He just got up and dusted himself off and came on in. He got a royal greeting, no doubt about that. We were just all glad he survived.

Red Sox infielder **Johnny Pesky:**

The first time they put on the shift, I didn't know what the hell was going on. They were running around like a bunch of chickens. I saw what they were trying to do. Ted just defied them. They gave him all of left field. Let him have a single. They wanted to keep the ball in the ballpark.

On the day we clinched, he hit a line drive to left center. The ball went all the way to the wall. In League Park, you had a long left field. He just kept running. Once he got on track, he could run. Ted, if he hit a ball to left field, it was an accident.

Defying popular wisdom, Yankees left-hander Tommy Byrne once brushed back Ted Williams before Ted even stepped up to the plate. **Byrne:**

They had a couple of men on. Casey [Stengel] brought me in. I can't recall who the pitcher was who I was relieving. There was an open base, and I had talked to Casey about what to do with Ted. He said, "Go ahead and get him out."

You normally take about six warm-up pitches. I had already taken about two or three. Ted was about six feet from home plate. He turned and he called Mickey Vernon, who was in the batter's circle, to come up there. They were watching me warm up. So I stood there for a moment. I thought that was interesting, that Ted didn't back off from where he was but called Mickey over to join him.

So I threw another pitch toward the plate. Yogi caught it. I assumed that Ted thought Casey told me to put him on and pitch to Vernon, so we'll have a force at every base. So Ted's trying to tell Vernon how my ball is moving. They're studying me. The point of it was, I didn't like that.

I didn't say a damn thing. What I did do was, after I threw one pitch in there and they got to collaborating, I decided I'd split their heads.

I threw one between them and hit the screen back there, and they both ducked. I almost got Williams and he called me an SOB and said, "If you had hit me with that goddamn ball, I would have thrown this bat at you." That was just fun for me, to watch 'em scatter. I missed them by about two feet each. Then I took a couple more warm-up pitches.

I pitched to Williams, and he hit a line drive off my shin. Fortunately, he couldn't run very fast. I got it over at the third-base line and threw him out, and the game was over. But he hit that ball pretty good. He wore my shin out.

Ted had a thing for All-Star Games, which is no surprise. He would deny it in booming tones, but Ted Williams was a closet showman. In the 1941 All-Star Game, he nearly leaped out of his shoes with joy as he rounded the bases on his game-winning, three-run home run in the bottom of the ninth in Detroit. **Doerr:**

I'd have to say that of all the thrills I had, that was probably the greatest thrill of seeing that home run. He was really excited about that. He was jumping up and down, which was unusual. That ball almost went completely out of the park.

In the 1946 All-Star Game, he was intrigued by the gimmick blooper pitch of Pittsburgh Pirates Rip Sewell. An intrigued Ted was dangerous. **Boo Ferriss:**

I was on the '46 American League All-Star team. We played the National League at Fenway Park.

He wasn't a bad fielder —when he put his mind to it. Ted was known to let a lousy mood or a bad at-bat distract him from his glove work. He once allowed a ball to roll around the outfield behind him while he examined his fingernails.

I just happened to be standing around the dugout when the National League was hitting before the game. I remember Ted hollering at Rip. He had never seen that blooper pitch before, and of course Rip got a lot of notoriety for it. He had been successful with it over in the National League.

Ted says, "Hey, Rip. You going to throw that thing today?" Rip says, "Yeah."

Ted says, "Boy, I want to hit at it. Throw that to me."

Ted went up to hit against him. It was the eighth inning, I believe. The first one went a little high. Ted took it. The next one was just about letter-high, that blooper pitch. I was in the right-field bullpen and the ball was coming right to us. At that time the Red Sox bullpen was on the right. I was standing on the pitcher's mound, watching that ball come. And I was going to catch it. My old left-handed teammate Mickey Harris jumped up in front of me and caught that ball.

Ted put on a great show that day. Ted got the pitch he wanted. He was just like a little kid after he hit it. That was the first time a home run had ever been hit off that blooper pitch.

Ted put on a show that day. Two home runs. And five RBIs. And he hit the first home run ever hit off of Rip Sewell's blooper pitch.

In the 1950 All-Star Game, Ted slammed into the outfield wall stealing a hit from Ralph Kiner. The collision wrecked Williams's elbow—doctors removed eight chips and various bone splinters— and handicapped his batting stroke for the rest of his career. Returning from the injury was one of the biggest challenges of his baseball life. Red Sox trainer **Jack Fadden:**

I've seen so many others go out of baseball with lesser ailments. Only a man with his great determination would ever come back to baseball—and tremendous baseball—as he did.

Let me try to draw a picture of the normal results of such an operation. The surgery was on the left elbow, the arm that follows through on his left-handed swing. Usually when you put your arms out in front of you full length, they are straight. After such an operation as Ted had, the left arm holds back, with a bend in the elbow.

But Williams worked and exercised furiously. Sometimes he nearly drove me nuts. I went to Florida a month early to give him additional exercises, morning and night, before the 1951 season. He drove himself as I've never seen a man work, before or since.

We worked all spring. He complained, surly and tough—but that's just a defense mechanism with him. There was a day in Sarasota he was pulling weights and he was irritated. I just laughed at him and told him that Walter Dropo was handling the same weights with ease. Well, that did it.

"If that big lug can do it, I can," Ted said. And he did.[5]

Yankees infielder **Jerry Coleman:**

He crashed into the wall at Comiskey Park. He hurt his elbow. He stayed in the game. He had a broken elbow, and he got a base hit.

It really ticked me off. I said, "Ted, you're hitting better with a broken arm than I can with a good arm." He actually chipped his elbow and got up and got a base hit.

I don't think anybody ever did that before.

Yankees manager **Casey Stengel,** *skipper of the '50 American League stars:*

I know many a so-and-so who has Williams marked lousy in his book. I hope they will all learn from this what a great guy he is. He didn't come back crying to me with his arm out like this and say, "I'm hurt. Get me out of there."

He said nothing. All I knew was that he backed up against the wall and made a helluva catch. If he had told me he was hurt, I would have got him out of there right away.

When I heard what had happened to Williams, I was sick.[6]

*Ted's only World Series was his biggest disappointment and most
bitter failure. In the greatest baseball show on Earth, he batted
.200 and the Red Sox fell to the St. Louis Cardinals in seven
games.* **Boo Ferriss:**

We clinched the pennant around the second week. The last
two weeks, we just played out the string. Tried to keep sharp.
The last day of the season, we were all packed up. We took
our suitcases to the ballpark, and we were going to catch the
late-afternoon train to St. Louis or Brooklyn. We were going
to start the World Series on Tuesday.

The National League ended in a tie. We had to go back
to our homes in Boston and wait until they had a playoff. It
was two out of three. The Series ended up not starting until
the following Sunday. Five days late.

Joe Cronin brought a bunch of American League All-
Stars to play against us, just to try to keep us sharp. Mickey
Haeffner, the little knuckleballer from Washington, hit Ted
on the right elbow. It hit right on the point. It wasn't on the
meat. It was on the bone.

Ted stayed in that whirlpool every day. He really wasn't
100 percent. It bothered him. But he never used it as an
excuse or anything.

Stan Musial hit .200, too. You don't hear much about
that, because they won.

Bobby Doerr:

I think the elbow was hurting him, but I don't think that was a big factor. It never really came out—every year Ted would get a virus. Almost like a flu. He got that about that time. He never did alibi about it. But he was feeling punk.

I'd been around him so many times when he'd had that happen to him. If it hadn't been a World Series, I don't think he would have played. Nothing was ever said about that. But he just wasn't sharp.

For the Cardinals to come out and say they knew how to pitch to him . . . Well, anything over the plate, Ted knew how to hit. It always made me a little disgusted that he got that bad virus in that World Series. His whole body was rubbed out.

Of all the things that happened in our career, to not play on a world championship team. We talked about it quite a bit, more since retirement.

His woeful World Series fueled Ted's critics, who said he could deliver when his batting average needed a hit but not when his team needed one. **Joe Cronin:**

I'd have to rate Ted with the top five clutch hitters who ever played. You take Babe Ruth, Lou Gehrig, and Joe DiMaggio, Jimmie Foxx and Harry Heilmann, and I put him right in the middle of the pack of them. I can't tell you about [Ty] Cobb, [Tris] Speaker, and others of a different day. I mean from my era.

In any given situation against any pitcher, Williams will do just as well at any time.

There have been many instances when a Williams hit had apparently won a ballgame for the Red Sox only to have some other department on the club crumble like a cookie so we lost it.[7]

Into the 1950s, with the Red Sox customarily out of the pennant race, Ted searched out other hurdles, such as batting titles, career records, and the most relentless opponent of all, middle age. Veteran first baseman **Mickey Vernon** *joined the Red Sox in 1956:*

That first year I was with Ted in Boston, he hit .388. It looked like he was going to hit .400. All the time he was leading the league, I was kidding him, because up until that point I was the oldest guy to lead the American League in hitting at the age of thirty-five. Ted and I are both the same age.

Now we were thirty-eight, and it looks like he's going to lead the league. He's a cinch to lead it. I said, "You just want to be the oldest guy to lead the league."

He said, "No, I just want to be number one, period. It doesn't make any difference where or when or how old."

Frank Malzone *joined the Red Sox full time in 1957, when Ted turned thirty-nine years old:*

I can remember that year, Ted and Pete Runnells, who was my roommate, they're going into the last day of the season fighting for the batting title.

We're in Washington, and Pete's got maybe a point lead on him going into the last day. Pete is hitting second in the lineup and Ted, as always, is hitting third.

Looking back, it's a bit funny, but I guess it wasn't funny to Pete Runnells. Pete, the first time up, gets a base hit. Ted comes up behind him—base hit.

I believe the second time up, Pete comes up and gets a double. So Ted says, what the hell, I might as well get a double, too.

Now, they're both 2-for-2. They're about even for the batting title. After Pete got his two hits and Ted got his second hit, me and Pete were sitting on the bench. Pete looks at me and I give him a little smile. He says, "You know what? I don't think he's going to let me win this batting title."

I looked at him and I said, "Pete, I don't think so, either."

That's just the competitiveness of Ted Williams.

Johnny Pesky:

When it got tough, he got tougher. I can still see him twisting his hands on that bat, just gritting his teeth. His cap—he'd pull his cap down over his eyes. One thing, too—he never got out of the batter's box. You see these guys take a pitch and walk around. He never did. He used to preach that to us: Never take your eye off the pitcher.

Birdie Tebbetts:

He could be compulsive. If I could hit like him, I wouldn't have thought about anything else, either.

He wanted to do everything. Have you got a pencil? Okay. He wanted to lead the league in batting average. He wanted to lead the league in base on balls. He wanted to lead the league in home runs. He wanted to lead the league in RBIs. He wanted to lead the league in (fewest) strikeouts.

He wanted to lead the league in everything. And I really believe, at any time during a game, he knew exactly where he stood in those categories.

One time, we went into Chicago to play a series. He was about three points behind Boudreau. I said to him before a doubleheader, "The Frenchman's got you" and walked away.

In the first game, he got 3-for-4. The fifth time up, he turned to me and said, "This one's for Ted." And he hit a home run.

He looked at me after the game and just grinned.[8]

On the day in 1952 when he said farewell to the Red Sox before leaving for Korea—he did not expect to survive the war—he homered in his last at bat. Perfect. On September 28, 1960, he played his final game at Fenway Park, and there was only one way Ted the closet showman wanted to bow out: perfectly, again.
Frank Malzone:

We all got wind of it, that this was going to be it. It was a typical fall day. Not too many people in the stands. Once we were out of the pennant race, we weren't drawing too well. Mike Higgins was the manager. I remember the second time up, he just missed hitting one. He flew out to right field. It was a tough day to hit a home run, because of the weather.

The third time up, he hit it in the bullpen. We were all clapping. The way he galloped around the bases—his gallop was something special when he hit a home run. As a youngster, he used to take long, leaping strides. But now as he got a little older, it was a different stride. Graceful. You knew it was Ted Williams, running.

When he got across home plate, he did like he always did—he put his head down. Like, "Ah, so what? I hit a home run." He runs in the dugout, figuring he was out of the game. We tried to get him to go out, and he went out a little bit. He stuck his head out, but he wouldn't go all the way out.

What happened was, he wasn't out of the game; Mike says, "You're still in left field." Ted went out and he went into left field, then Mike sent somebody out to replace him.

And Ted had to come in, in front of the people. His last hurrah was running in. Again, his typical little stride, with his head down.

I think it was a little emotional for him, although he hated to admit those things. We wanted to shake his hand, but we didn't get the chance. Before you know it, he's in the clubhouse.

Red Sox teammate **Ray Boone:**

I knew he was going to hit one. Those kinds of guys always do stuff like that.

After Ted hit the home run, he went into the clubhouse. The fans started throwing cushions on the field, because they wanted Ted to come out. They knew it was his last at bat, and they stood and cheered for him like you wouldn't believe.

The umpires came over and they said, "We're not going to get this game going unless you bring Ted out."

So Ted came out and waved to the fans. And they proceeded to get the cushions off the field.

Maureen Cronin:

It was overcast. It was cold. We knew ahead of time that it was his last game. We really weren't surprised when he hit the home run. You just expected him to be Mr. Wonderful.

When he hit the home run, it was just electrifying. I remember not being surprised.

Ted loved the show, forever. **George Sullivan:**

I became the Red Sox PR director in October 1981. One of the first things I wanted to do was put in Old-Timers games. The Red Sox have such a great history and such a great array of stars.

After I tried it out on the owners and they said yes, then I decided to try it out on Ted Williams. Because if he said no, then I would question whether we should even have it. If we have an Old-Timers Day and he doesn't come, it sort of takes the heart out of the Old-Timers Day. It would be an embarrassment.

So I call him in Florida. Naturally, you can't get him directly. But I left a message with the right person. And he called me right back.

I said, "You're going to love me."

He said, "Yuh, yuh, yuh, what else is new?"

"We're going to have an Old-Timers game."

He really went crazy. He said, "You know me. I have always said that I'd never play in an Old-Timers game."

I did what I had learned to do with him. I held the phone out and let him rant for five minutes, knowing his last sentence would be, "When do you want me there?" And that's just what he did.

We had the game in '82. I have never seen such reaction. I knew I'd be besieged for tickets, but from young people—guys who had been born years after Ted Williams retired. They were the ones as much as the old-timers who wanted to see Williams. I was just amazed at how he drew attention from young people. I guess they must have heard so much about him. But the media went nuts, too.

I had Ted's team hit first. Ted batted in the first inning and went out into left field. Mike Andrews led off the bottom of the first, and he hit a sinking line drive to left field. And here comes Ted. I can still see him galloping in. Just like the old days, galloping with that lope of his.

And he made a catch right off his shoetops. One of those ice-cream-cone catches. But he couldn't stop, and he couldn't brake himself, and here he comes. I thought he was going to fall and I could see the headlines the next day: WILLIAMS BREAKS HIS COLLARBONE. He ended up on the skin of the infield.

The funny thing was, he didn't get a hit. I'm thinking to myself, *It's not surprising that Williams comes out a headliner at*

Old-Timers Day, but who would have thought it would be for his fielding?

After the game I go into the locker room just after the Red Sox are coming into the field to play their regular game. So it's just the old-timers and they're all huddled around Williams. He was still in uniform in the middle of the locker room. Here I come into the room, and he sees me. He says, "You son of a bitch, I've been waiting for you." He seemed a little bit upset. He said, "We've got to have a talk."

So I say, "Let's go into [Red Sox manager Ralph] Houk's office." So we go into Houk's office.

He shuts the door. He said, "You know, when you called me last fall, I told you the last thing I ever wanted to do was play in an Old-Timers game. And I woke up this morning at the Sheraton-Boston and I looked in the mirror and I said, 'Jesus Christ, what am I doing here? This is going to be one of the worst days of my life.' Were your ears ringing? Because I was cursing you.

"Now, I want to tell you something. I'm going to tell you to your face. This was one of the great days of my life."

TWO TEDS

I always figured Ted was like a [George S.] Patton. Everything forward, no reverse, no retreat, no compromise. The other side of him was a very, very thoughtful and compassionate person.
—BOBBY DOERR

Ted Williams—surprise—hated to be psychoanalyzed. He didn't want to hear about persecution complexes, inferiority complexes, overcompensation, personality disorders—and who can blame him? Sometimes a bat is just a bat, and sometimes a glib, explosive, charming, intelligent, maddening bundle of contradictions is just . . . Ted Williams.

A lot of people have two sides to them. Ted's two sides just happened to be total opposites.

He was a pal with the press, and he was brutally heartless with the press. He was a charming gentleman, and he had a notorious foul mouth. He had a voice like a howitzer, and he was gently sweet with children. He was sarcastic, and he was sensitive. He was an intelligent grownup, and he threw tantrums like a spoiled kid. He was a chatterbox, and he was a loner.

He was a rebel—he refused to tip his cap, he refused to wear a tie, he did everything his way—and he was an ardent Republican.

He acted as if he didn't need love from the fans, and he acted hurt and angry when he didn't get it.

He was a happy, zestful man who was curious about life and adventure. And he was a nervous perfectionist with deep passion—the formula for great torment.

In one respect, though, Ted's personality made complete sense. He hated to be bored, so he was never boring.

Long-time friend and San Diego native **Frank Cushing:**

His mom was quite an interesting woman. She meant well. She was with the Salvation Army. Everybody knew her. I'd see her on the streetcars. I'd see her on the No. 11 streetcar. They lived on Utah Street. She was a nice person, but she was thoroughly dedicated to getting donations for the Salvation Army, to the extent that it made it a little difficult for the two boys, Ted and his younger brother, Danny.

I didn't know Danny at all. He was a pack of trouble. He was constantly a thorn in everybody's side. Everybody knew of him. He had a reputation for being antisocial. He got in trouble later on in Chicago. He was a source of difficulty for Ted.

I never knew his dad. His dad spent most of his time up in Sacramento. He moved and had a photography business.

The things that Ted talked about mainly were the good things that happened to him. A guy named Rod Luscomb, who was the playground director, who took Ted under his wing, who was kind of a second father to him and helped him on his early baseball stuff. And Coach [Wos] Caldwell at Hoover. He talks about all the people who helped him.

I never heard him say an unkind word about his mother or father. He really was just fortunate that he had this obsession with baseball. And had some nice friends. Les Cassie was one of them.

His brother didn't have anything special. When two kids are left alone at home most of the time, the propensity for difficulty is there. But Ted was so obsessed with baseball, he spent every spare moment trying to get Rod Luscomb or somebody to pitch balls to him. Ted was not trouble-prone. Danny was just a punk.

We were stationed together at the Marine Corps air station at Ewa Field in Hawaii toward the end of World War II. I really didn't get to know him well until we both came back from Korea. A very close friend of mine who flew in VMF-311, which Ted was in, a guy by the name of Jim Stehle, was very close to Ted. I was up in the front lines as an infantry officer.

When I came back from Korea in the fall of '53, my friend Jim said, "Why don't we go up to the Washington Senators game?" We went up and saw a game and we met with Ted after the game at the old Griffith Stadium. We met, and he said, "Gosh, you look familiar." We became close friends.

I remember after I got out of the Marine Corps, I was a college professor down at the University of Louisville. Ted heard that I was hospitalized. He called my wife and said, "I don't know what your insurance situation is, but for God's sake, if you need any money, if there's anything I can do, give me a call." He was just the most generous person in the world.

The time I spent the most time with him was 1991. He and I went on a cruise together for fifteen days. He and his long-time companion, Louise Kaufman, met us in Acapulco and spent three or four days there and got on the ship and went through the Panama Canal.

When we were on the cruise, the cruise director asked me, "Do you think there would be any possibility that Ted would be willing somewhere toward the end of the cruise to give a talk in the lounge?" I said, "I can sure ask him."

I talked to Ted. He said, "I don't think anybody would come. I'd be embarrassed. I doubt anybody would even show up."

Well, when the day came and it was announced and put on the ship's schedule, everyone on the ship—except maybe one guy in the engine room and maybe one guy on the bridge—everyone from the captain to the laundryman was there. They had an overflow crowd. Ted was flabbergasted. He didn't think anyone would show up.

It was scheduled for forty-five minutes. After the time was up, he answered questions for another twenty or thirty minutes. And then he agreed to go to the rear and spent the better part of an hour signing autographs and taking pictures.

One of the last places we stopped was St. Thomas. Ted, Lou, and I were in this little café. Ted was going to pay the bill, and Lou and I kind of walked outside. The place was filled, but nobody said anything to Ted.

When Ted got up, everybody gave him a huge ovation. Just a spontaneous thing, in St. Thomas of all places.

I've known all three of his wives. Doris was a really nice gal. She was his first wife. He had one daughter, Bobby Jo, by Doris. Doris was just a small-town gal from Minnesota. He met her when he was playing in 1938 in Minneapolis. They divorced in 1955. They were both very young.

In the late '50s, he married Lee. I only met her a couple of times. She was a real nice person from Chicago. They were married for a very short time. She was very nice, but she couldn't have been more different than Ted. She was a very sophisticated person and I think she loved Ted. I know Doris did, too. But they had such a different lifestyle. She was a big-city girl from Chicago. I think she had done some modeling. And Ted was gone most of the time. Ted and Curt Gowdy would go off to Australia and other places. I think she loved Ted, and Ted in his own way loved her, but they did split up.

Then he married Delores. He had his other two children with Delores, Claudia and John Henry. They ultimately split up. They weren't meant for each other. Ted was probably not the easiest dude to ever live with. But he was good to all of them.

The one I knew best was Bobby Jo, his first child, his daughter. I'm still very close to Bobby Jo and her husband. Ted really loved Bobby Jo, and Bobby Jo adored Ted, but Bobby Jo had her problems early on. That used to drive Ted up the wall. But she has straightened out and they've become very close. She moved in the last few years down to Crystal River so she could be near Ted. They've got a very close relationship.

There were times when he was concerned about her. He was so grateful in his later years that they had a close relationship. It wasn't always easy, because Ted wasn't always available to her. But she always loved Ted. And expressing love wasn't always easy for Ted, but he told me many times how proud he was of how things went for Bobby Jo.

Ted and Louise Kaufman knew each other in a friendly capacity for years down in Islamorada. She was married to Bob Kaufman. They never had any relationship until well after Bob died. They started dating about a year after Bob Kaufman died. They became a couple, then they became an item. I'd say in about '78 or '79. But they knew each other, and she knew Ted's lifestyle and his idiosyncrasies. They had a good friendship, and they ultimately lived together.

Ted was what you would term a man's man. I think where Delores and Lee found it difficult to get used to that, I think Louise understood that. He was very good to Louise. I can't say that I didn't see occasions when they shouted at each other. But most of the time when he would, he'd look at me and wink. And two minutes later, it would be back to normal.

Ted used to spend the summers in New Brunswick. He would get awfully hot in the summer in the Florida Keys, and he used to spend the summers in New Brunswick. Louise Kaufman used to stay with him. She was his long-time companion. They never married, but she was the only gal that really loved Ted. They really had a great relationship. I spent a lot of time in Citrus Hills with them. When they started living together, they bought a place up in Citrus Hills. She was a real great gal. And they got along just great.

She passed away just before Ted had his first stroke. It occurred when they were up in Canada, in New Brunswick. She had an obstruction and they got her to the hospital, but it was too late. It was very severe. She died in a matter of a few days.

It was very difficult when he lost Louise. I went down to see him in Citrus Hills shortly after Louise passed away. He was really very devastated. I think she was really the only good solid relationship. She loved him and he loved her.

Long-time friend and teammate **Bobby Doerr:**

He always had the Dr. Jekyll personality. You saw the movie *Patton*. I always figured Ted was like a Patton. Everything forward, no reverse, no retreat, no compromise. Everything forward, very positive-thinking guy. There's no negative at all. And there's very little compromise. Very sharp. I think he could have been a great general or a great whatever.

He was such a sharp guy. He didn't understand mediocrity, which is what about 90 percent of us have. To me, it was too hard to be a perfectionist.

The other side of him was a very, very thoughtful and compassionate person. He would do anything in the world for anybody.

You knew that he didn't have a very good family home life. But you didn't know that it was a setup where, as he told me later, that a lot of times he'd go home and make some scrambled eggs and bacon for meals and there would be nobody there.

He used to tell me so many times, "You're so lucky, Bobby, to have a mom and dad like you have." He admired my folks. He'd come and have dinner with us sometimes. My folks would come down almost every weekend to San Diego to watch us play. He could see the love effect in our family. He didn't have it.

Ted and I were real close. There would be times when he would get letters. You could just see him reading this letter and all of a sudden he would just tear it up and throw it in the can. You knew that he got a letter from his mother. His mother was always asking for money from Ted to try to bail his brother out of problems. You knew Ted was disgusted about that. You knew he was sending money to his mother, but you knew she was giving it to Ted's brother.

One time after we got through playing ball, I think it was 1961, we went down to San Diego. We had lunch. Then he said, "I want to show you guys where my dad's photography studio used to be." It was about two blocks from where we ate. When he was walking up the stairs, you could imagine a little kid, about seven, eight, nine years old, walking up these stairs.

When we walked back down, and we're right on this corner of the street, he says, "Right there is where my mom used to make me walk behind the Salvation Army band. I used to crouch down behind the big bass drum to try to hide."

I thought at the time, *That's where all that fighting embarrassment comes from.* Right there on that corner, he was just like a little kid reminiscing about things.

In San Diego, after he joined the club, we were on a train trip. The regular players had lower berths. The irregulars and the extra pitchers had upper berths. When you would be going on one of those trips, a few of the older players would have a few drinks and they'd come in. This one night, they were gigging Ted up in the upper berth. Ribbing him and gigging him and so forth. He finally took a blanket and wrapped it around himself and went into the women's restroom and went in the toilet and locked himself in so they couldn't get to him.

One time we were in Oakland. Your meal money I think was two dollars. We used to go to movies almost every night. If there was a western movie, we'd go to the movie together. He and I had been to a movie and came back to the hotel in Oakland. There was kind of a runway going into the lobby of the hotel, and Mr. Lane, he had kind of a grouchy voice.

He kind of grabbed Ted by the arm and he says, "Son, you're heading the list."

Ted says, "What list?"

"The overeaters. You're eating over the limit."

Ted says, "I can't eat on that measly two-dollar-a-day meal money."

He was very hyper. He was always chewing his fingernails. Upbeat all the time. We were in Sacramento this one time. He ate around three, three-thirty, so when he went to the ballpark, he wouldn't be full of food. He came into the counter in the restaurant. I was sitting at a table with some guys. Ted pounded on the counter and he was saying, "Waitress, I've got to catch a train." He was just trying to get the waitress to give him a hurry-up meal. That's the way he was. Everything was quick. Bang, bang. He wasn't going to go anywhere, he just wanted to get his food quick and get out of there.

When we'd go to Cleveland or Detroit, you'd always get to town, traveling by train, maybe nine-thirty or so. He'd always say, "Come on, Bobby. Let's go take a walk."

He loved to go around and look at window displays. They had pretty nice displays in those different department stores. We'd talk fishing and stuff like that. Or he'd say, "Bobby, I don't know why you can't hit more than .300 every year." He'd kid me about that.

But he always would like to be one-on-one. One night, Walt Masterson said, "What are you guys going to do?" We said we were going to take a walk. He said, "Do you mind if I go?" Ted said, "You guys go ahead and go." He didn't want a third person in on it.

He's a very, very compassionate guy. My God, at any time that I've known Ted, if I said, "Ted, I need ten thousand dollars. I can't explain to you what it's for. I just need it." It wouldn't have been any problem. He was that kind of guy. I just felt that.

He did a lot of things after ball games that people didn't know about. Going to hospitals. Going into the stands. But he didn't want anyone to know about it. He didn't want any fanfare.

*Long-time friend **Bob Breitbard:***

I first met Ted in February of 1934. We were at Hoover High School in San Diego together. He played baseball and I played football. We were in many classes together. He always happened to sit right behind me. Of course, I liked it that way, because he was so tall.

You know, they always kid Ted about not wearing a tie. He did wear a tie to our prom. And we double-dated. He took a young lady, and we had a good time. He did wear a tie.

We graduated from high school in February 1937. They had the ceremony in front of the student body, out in front of the school. When I say the student body, the students would look out from the windows. Floyd Johnson, the principal of the school, after we went through everything, he says, "Now, I have two awards to present. One to Ted Williams and one to Bob Breitbard. For typing thirty-two words a minute without an error." That was our claim to fame.

We spent a lot more time together after he retired. Two years ago, we went back when they had the All-Star Game at Fenway Park. That was the most fabulous thing I've ever seen. All the players came from the outfield, like in *Field of Dreams*. They came from the outfield in groups, and they lined up from home to first, first to second, second to third, third to home. And then Ted came in and there was a standing ovation for Ted coming out.

He threw out the first ball, and he got it over the plate. I'll tell you, everybody in the whole place was crying. They could have done without the All-Star Game, because that's all they needed.

Without a necktie but still looking dapper, Ted with Jackie Robinson. Ted's tieless look became a trademark and a symbol of his reputation for living life on his own terms.

We were at the hotel together. He couldn't get over it. The fans. The standing ovation when he came onto the field in a wheelchair. It was a wonderful feeling.

The next day, we went over to the hospital, where they have the Jimmy Fund. We walked into the hospital, and it seemed to me that there were fifteen hundred nurses and doctors lined in the hallways, and we wheeled Ted in. They were giving him a standing ovation.

They took us to where there was a little youngster, his head shaved, about nine months old, in the arms of his mother. Ted stops his wheelchair. The mother and father are there. Ted rubbed the youngster's head and says, "That young man is going to be okay. You believe me. He's . . . going . . . to . . . be . . . okay. You can mark my words."

We kept on going. There must have been forty youngsters in this room, all with cancer. Ted has a little thing that he does with young people. He's very perceptive. There are two youngsters standing there. He'll say to one of them, "I'll betcha I can tell you how old you are." And the kid says, "Yeaah. How old do you think I am?" Ted says, "We-e-e-e-l-l-l-l, I think you're either nine . . . or ten. And I think you're ten years old."

The kid says, "Yup. I am. I'm ten years old."

And Ted says, "Okay. How old do you think I am?"

The kid looks at him and says, "About 110."

Ted loves kids.

Les Cassie Jr.:

We were friends in high school. It wasn't very long before I had him come over to my house. I went over to his house. He and my dad got to be real good friends. They used to go surf fishing together. I went with them one time and thought it was the most boring thing that I had ever done.

My dad and Ted used to go down to Mission Valley and they used to go into the bushes where they'd get poles, bamboo poles. They'd cut them and bring them back to our house so he and my dad could make their own poles. They were good friends.

One time I was over to his house after he had signed and played with the Padres in '36. We were sitting at his house and the phone rang. He answered it in a pretty loud voice: "HELLO." The guy said who it was. It was Dick Ward, who was the pitcher with the Padres. He was selling cars. He wanted to sell Ted a car.

All of a sudden, Ted put the phone down and he started to laugh. I said, "What are you laughing about?" Ted said, "Dick told me to hang up the phone. He could hear me just as well without it."

Ted got a letter telling him to report to spring training on such-and-such a date. And they sent him a bus ticket from San Diego to Sarasota, Florida. He decided to ask my dad to go with him. My dad said, "Sure, I'll go with you."

They rode the bus, and in New Orleans, Ted got sick as the dickens. They had to get off the bus, get a hotel, and my dad had to nurse him back to health.

When Ted came back from the service in '46, he came over to the house, and we got to talking about baseball. He told my mother and dad, "If we get into the Series in the next five years, I'm going to call you up and have you come back as my guests at the World Series."

They won it in '46, and sure enough, the night they clinched the pennant, he called my dad. He treated my dad so nice. He was so good to him while the Series was going on. He introduced my dad to everybody from Mr. Yawkey down to the clubhouse boy and the ushers in the ballpark.

It was one of the high spots of my dad's life.

Joe Villarino:

I was about six and he was about seven, and we used to play marbles together. We used to play at the North Park playground. We had holes in our pants at the knees from resting on the ground. He was good. He wanted to excel at everything—even marbles.

He had a nice little house. He lived with his mom and dad. Finally, his mom and dad separated. She was in the Salvation Army, you know. He used to come home to an empty house most of the time. His mother used to stay out working for the Salvation Army, out until ten or eleven o'clock at night. I knew her real well. She'd have me over for dinner once in a while. She was a fine lady.

She loved to talk. She was kind of a religious woman, too. Every time I saw her, she had on that Salvation Army uniform. She'd get somebody cornered on the bus. I hope you don't say too much about that, because I don't think Ted liked that too well.

Ray Boone, *of San Diego and the major leagues:*

Ted's mother worked for the Salvation Army. I saw her around all the time. She'd always be on the corner at Christmastime, ringing her bell. We'd see her in the buses, and she'd be talking religion.

We'd see her all over. We'd say, "There's Ted's mother." And sometimes she would remind us that Ted Williams was her son. She was a nice lady. She just knew she was dedicated to the Salvation Army. That was her whole life.

When I was with Cleveland, I remember the first time Ted came to town. I was warming up for infield practice. I was maybe twenty feet from the batting cage, and Ted was standing there. I was thinking, *Should I go over and tell him I went to Hoover High?* Then I thought not to. *What if he says, "Yeah, who cares?"*

Later, I had one of my better days at Fenway Park. I hit two home runs on a Saturday. On Sunday, I was making the third out in an inning. I was on my way to shortstop. Ted was on his way in from left field. We passed each other. I'm not going to say anything.

He said, "They can't get old Hoover out, can they?"

I never will forget that.

Floyd Johnson, principal of Hoover High School in San Diego:

He habitually stopped in the office to have a friendly chat with the principal who, to him, was not a superior person, but just another man and a friend.

As these little visits progressed, the conversation always turned to baseball and fishing, and I always have been extremely interested in both sports. Often Ted would ask me if I were ready to go fishing. If one had looked in on one of those visits, they would have seen Ted slumped down in a chair with his feet on the principal's desk. I was completely oblivious of Ted's posture. I thoroughly enjoyed the conversation. This was not impudence on Ted's part, because to him all folks on campus were just the same—faculty, principal, or kids.[1]

Minneapolis outfielder **Joe Gallagher:**

One afternoon, Ted was having a bad time. He let two balls go through him. He struck out twice. After he fanned for what he thought was his final time at bat, he retired to the clubhouse without being ordered to do so by Bush.

As he undressed, the Millers staged a rally. There were two out and two on. A batboy was sent back to the clubhouse to get Williams. Ted got dressed and came out and hit a home run.

During a batting slump, Ted wanted to quit and go back to San Diego. He was all packed when Donie Bush, who was our manager, heard about it. Donie called Ted into his office.

"Ted, I will arrange for your transportation home, and after you have visited the folks, you can come back."

Williams had expected Bush to raise hell. The manager's acceptance of the situation took all the wind out of his sails. He didn't go to San Diego.[2]

Pitcher **Charlie Wagner,** *Red Sox teammate:*

We became very good friends. He got up early and I got up early. We didn't drink or smoke. No nightclubs and all that stuff. We became roommates.

Ted liked company, but he was a loner in a sense. He liked company when he wanted company. We lived at the same hotel in Boston. It was the Sheraton Hotel on Bay State Road. It was the nicest hotel. It had a roof garden. I used to go in there and sit in the corner and watch people come in. It was a nice hotel. You could hide away there, and nobody would know it. Ted would fly out and fly back. He liked to do things alone. But he had every friend in America.

He had guys who used to sell him newspapers down in Kenmore Square. He had a guy who he used to take care of like a little boy. He'd talk to him. "Yeah, sure. What's in the paper today? What did they say about me today?" He'd chat with everybody. He wasn't aloof. He got along with everybody. He never had a bad talk with anybody. He never ignored anybody.

He wouldn't wear a tie. He'd never wear a tie. He dressed well, and he looked well—just without a tie. We were in Washington one time, and we went in to eat. All these senators and generals were there. It was a classy place. They wouldn't let him in because he didn't have a tie. Ted said, "Well, this is enough of this goddamn blah-blah-blah." He turned to me and said, "Let's go up to the room and order something." That's what we did.

He was a nervous type of guy. He had energy up to the hilt. He got the hives one night. He woke me up around three-thirty in the morning. I heard a few "son of a bitches." I said, "Let me call the doc." Ted has got the hives, and he's scratching all over the place.

Then the doctor comes in. Ted is scratching away. So now they give him adrenaline. That makes you nervous as hell. It makes you jumpy. He went out of his gourd. "Holy Christ!" he was saying. "What the hell is wrong with me!" The last thing he needed was adrenaline.

He was always in a hurry. Going nowhere. Whoosh, out the door. Well, it got rid of the hives. He was up all night. He was bitching and moaning. And we played the next day. And Ted did very good.

He was nuts on cowboy movies. John Wayne. I asked him once who would he want to play him in the movies if they made a movie about him. He said, "John Wayne." And I said, "Well, who would you want to play my part? You know, your roomie and everything?" He said, "Mickey Rooney." He used to take shots at me all the time. It was all in fun.

*Pitcher **Eldon Auker,** Red Sox teammate:*

He was always just a lot of fun. Laughing and joking. A real bright personality. Everybody liked him.

I roomed with Jimmie Foxx on the road. Jimmie was living in the same hotel in Boston as Ted and a couple of the other guys. Three or four times during the season, we had Ted and Jimmie come out for my wife's fried chicken. Ted was always excited about that. He was just a great kid. A kid at heart, really.

You know, in those days, we always wore a suit and a tie. We always had a necktie. In fact, in Detroit, Mickey Cochrane had a fifty-dollar fine if we came to the ballpark on the road or at home or to the hotel without a coat and a tie. He said, "You're major-leaguers; you want to look like major-leaguers." We never wore open-neck shirts. I think Ted was probably one of the first ones to break that rule. The reason for it is because he just wouldn't spend any money on himself.

Outfielder **Sam Mele,** *Red Sox teammate 1947–49, 1954–55:*

I met Ted when I was going to New York University, and my coach down there, Bill McCarthy, was very friendly with Neil Mahoney, who was a Red Sox scout. Bill McCarthy used to drive me up to Fenway Park so I could work out with the Red Sox.

Al Simmons was with the club at the time. They told me as a rookie, "Go in and take five swings." So I took four, or whatever it was. And Simmons says, "Hey, how many you gonna hit?" It made me shudder. Here was a great player, and he's saying more or less, "Get the hell out of there."

Later, I'm taking batting practice and I'm hitting the ball pretty good. I swung at a pitch. The next pitch, I didn't swing at. And a voice behind the cage says, "Well, why didn't you hit that ball?" I said, "Well, I think it was low." The voice said, "It had part of the plate anyway." So now when I got out of the cage, I'm introduced to the voice. It was Ted Williams who was saying that to me. One minute, Al Simmons is telling me to get out of there, the next minute Ted Williams is being nice.

He invited me a number of times to his house for supper. He would go down in the basement and have me go with him, and he would tie flies for fishing. That started the friendship. I didn't like fishing at all. He was a master at it. But Ted, as big as he was, and I'm only a rookie—if he asked you to do something, you wanted to do it.

My wife and I invited Ted to our house in Quincy one time. He loved pasta, okay? Ted came to the house, and we're sitting down eating pasta. All of a sudden, the doorbell is ringing and there's a bunch of kids outside. Somehow they found out he was there. So I went to the door and I said, "No, leave the man alone."

Ted says, "No, let them in. That's all right." He told them to form a line. He had them come in, go around the table to where he was and he would sign an autograph on whatever they had, and go right out the front door. He did that for fifteen, twenty minutes. He signed every one.

This I know. He was very generous. People used to write to his secretary, needy people I'm talking about. He would tell his secretary: "Send this one ten dollars, send that one twenty dollars." He always helped out. And for the Jimmy Fund, he was fantastic. And he wanted no fanfare, nothing.

He was sentimental in a way. I asked him if he would sign an autograph for my father. He wrote, "To Tony Mele, you have one great son, Sam. Ted Williams." You know what I always thought about Ted? He was a little bit of a softy, but he wanted people to think he was tough, hardhearted. He would do nice things, but he didn't want people to know he was that nice.

Ted always liked to box. You know, just throw up your hands and fool around. He was a great boxing fan to begin with. He took in a lot of fights.

This is 1948. We were on the train one day, and he's coming toward me and I'm coming toward him, and we happen to meet where there was a men's room or something, and the aisle was smaller. He puts up his hands. I put up my hands, and we spar a little bit. He goes by. I go by.

The next morning, I'm eating breakfast. Paul Schreiber, who was our batting practice pitcher and Ted's roommate, comes over to my table and says, "What did you do to Ted?"

I said, "What do you mean?" He said, "We had the doctor up there." Well, anyway, what happened was, I separated a rib from a cartilage. Which was accidental, of course. And he missed three weeks in '48. And that's the year we tied Cleveland.

And I'm figuring, in three weeks, he could have won four, five, six games for us. And we'd have been a shoo-in for the pennant. But they beat us in the playoff game. I don't know if I hit him just right or if he turned wrong, but that was the result of it.

I was traded the next June. I can't say it was because of that. Joe McCarthy was a great Williams fan. But I can't say that. The reason I got traded was, McCarthy wanted Walter Masterson, because he pitched very well against the Yankees. He was more of what could help the ball club, not because of that.

When I was fired as manager in Minnesota, Bob Short called me. He was the owner of the Washington ball club. He wanted me to manage there. I said, "Geez, I had enough." It bothered me an awful lot, managing. I'm not thick-skinned. So he hired Ted Williams.

So I go into Fenway Park during the season to say hello to him. And Ted looks at me in his office and says, "Why the hell didn't you take the job?"

I said, "Why?"

He's got these tablets for your stomach. He said, "If you had taken this job, I wouldn't be taking these."

Remember the time they had that big night for Ted at the Wang Center? I think this was in 1988. Dom DiMaggio was there, John Glenn was there, Joe DiMaggio was there.

The next night, in Quincy, at the neighborhood club, they had a night for me. I walk in the place, and they said, "Let's go downstairs." I start down the stairs, and there's Ted Williams, Bobby Doerr, [Eddie] Pellegrini, [Walt] Dropo. Doerr and Williams stayed overnight after that thing at the Wang Center to come to my thing. In Quincy. At the neighborhood club. I could have cried.

*Pitcher **Mel Parnell,** Red Sox teammate:*

You know, Ted was the kind of person that during batting practice, if there was a pitch that he could hit right back through the middle, he would take the pitch. He didn't want to take a chance on hurting the batting practice pitcher. That's the way he was. He was a gentle, kindhearted person.

*Boston Braves outfielder **Max West:***

We were on that train ride to his first spring training with the Red Sox. I don't know why he did this, because I don't think he had even seen Joe Cronin. I don't know. But on the train, he kept saying all the time, "If Joe Cronin thinks he's going to tell me what to do, he's full of you-know-what." Cronin was the manager then. He didn't know Cronin from a hole in the wall.

We trained in Bradenton, and the Red Sox trained in Sarasota. We were over there one day, and Jimmie Foxx and all those other guys would hit and just stand around the cage. So old Ted, he thought he'd do that, too. Instead of hitting and running around the bases, like you normally do, and go out and field some, he just stood around with Foxx and Cronin and all those guys. He was a rookie, and he was standing around with the veterans. He thought he should stand around, too.

There were so many things over the years. I remember during the season that was the anniversary of the baseball centennial. This was in 1969. Quite a few of us old players were invited to Washington. A four- or five-day celebration. This was a big, big thing. The day of the All-Star Game, it rained like crazy. It poured. So we were at the White House. There's thirty or forty ballplayers. They checked us in. We went in, and there was nobody else in there. They had refreshments and food. They took us in the ballroom, and we met Richard Nixon. We were all gathered in a circle near this ramplike thing to go up and be introduced to the president. Casey Stengel was standing on one side of me, and I looked around, and there was Ted. He wasn't with us. I said, "How did you get in here?" About that time, they called us up to meet the president. And when we got down, I looked around for Ted, and he was gone. Just disappeared. How he got into the White House and out of the White House, I don't know.

Tony Lupien played first base with the Red Sox for one full season in 1942:

To me, if I were to write a book about the man, I would say he's a great hitter. Period.

The memories that I might have might not be too palatable to the general public. The things I might say might not add any joy to anybody's life.

One memory that quickly comes to mind. Mrs. Yawkey had a dinner for us about the time we were in the game together. This was when we were all done. This was in Boston. At that time, Ted said this: "I didn't realize what a good bunch of guys I played with until it was all over."

That's a hell of a statement to make. If you had no more knowledge of the people that you were working with than that, you didn't have a great deal of a grasp on, not only human nature, but the people that you were doing business with. I think by expressing to Mrs. Yawkey what he did, that he was expressing regret for the way he has lived his life.

He took care of Ted very well. That's the way life has been with that man.

*Dr. **Sidney Farber** was leader of the Jimmy Fund, the pediatric cancer institute to which Ted Williams was deeply devoted.*

There's a man running a hundred yards in two seconds and he steps on a little pebble, falls down and breaks his neck. The same man walking a hundred yards at leisure would never notice the pebble.

There's that tremendous drive to strive to do so well. That intenseness, that strive toward perfection.

Now if you should get up from that chair and punch your fist through that window, I wouldn't think you were a bad man. I would want to discover the precipitating cause. There must be something that makes a fine human being do something he really doesn't want to do.

I believe that any performer, whether he be a violinist or an artist—doing something the rest of the world isn't doing—has to have tremendous concentration. He's not to be regarded as a person just sitting and observing.

You remember the stories about General Patton. I deplore anything that was ever said against him. He was a man of greatness under a strain.

From my own personal viewpoint, I can't understand why fans boo Ted at times. Here's a man with a greatness as an athlete. If he bats .400, which is considered as near to perfection as a player can get, it also means that he has failed 600 times. I think that we should remember the .400 and not dwell on the rest.[3]

The Most Reverend **Richard J. Cushing,** *archbishop of Boston:*

He's fighting and winning the toughest battle of them all—the fight against himself. He's had a battle all the way. I've seen him grow. I think he's winning it.

I don't know anything about his background. But if he had received the preparation, if he had the higher education, if he had the social contacts, this fellow would be an outstanding man in any field.

He has had to wage this war against himself.

Some men have to fight the battle of intemperance. Not Ted. Some have to fight against smoking. Not Ted. I have great admiration for his accomplishments in his war against himself.

He has had to conquer innate shyness, and he is a very shy man, his impatience, his tendency to be irritable when he says things he never meant to say.

I think the Jimmy Fund has worked two ways. Like a door that swings both ways. The fund has been helped considerably by Ted and it, in turn, has helped Ted. It has worked for the benefit of both. He has told me that. He has told me about the deep impression it has made on him.

I think that Dr. Farber has been a tremendous influence on Ted in winning this battle against himself. Ted has studied

Dr. Farber, dedicated in life to relieve those who suffer at the mercy of cancer. The calm, unostentatious doctor, going about his work with endless devotion, has registered with Ted. Ted has told me that. He has been powerfully influenced.[4]

*Lt. Col. **Patrick Harrison,** who served with Ted in Korea, took in a Red Sox game at Fenway Park in 1956:*

I went to the clubhouse to see Ted. We talked for a minute, then he threw me the keys to the hotel room.

"Why don't you go down there, make yourselves at home. I'll join you in a little while," Ted said. "Oh, yeah, I'm expecting a couple of guests. If they come before I get there, just introduce yourselves and tell them I'll be right along."

So we went to the hotel, up to the room, and we took Ted at his word. We made ourselves at home. It was just a matter of minutes when there was a knock on the door and I thought, "The guests are arriving." I went to the door.

The guests? A little girl, she couldn't have been more than 15 years old, with her mother, a mayor, and a police chief from some small town in Connecticut.

The little girl was on crutches. She had lost a leg just above the knee. She'd written to Ted. He invited her to visit.

Well, Ted joined us shortly after that and he sat talking with that little girl for a long time, just as if there was no others in the room. This was better for her than Christmas. Her eyes sparkled. Her face flushed. Here was no little girl, commiserating with herself. She was an inspired youngster who, for a time at least, forgot her misfortune. Leaving that apartment after a long visit, she was in a happy trance.[5]

Lew Powers *recalls attending civilian pilot training courses at Amherst in the winter of 1942:*

Most of the fellows there were from Boston, except for the ballplayers—Williams, Johnny Sain, Buddy Gremp, Johnny Pesky. Joe Coleman of Natick was in the same class.

Everybody had gone home for Christmas. Everybody but the ballplayers. I stayed, too. I didn't have any money, and there wasn't much point to it.

I bumped into Williams in the fraternity house where we were living. He asked me in that big, bluff way of his, "No home to go to?" I just passed it off, something to the effect that I was broke, and let it go at that.

He wouldn't let go. He forced money into my hand, a couple of hundred dollars, and told me in no uncertain terms to get the hell out of there.

I tried to tell him I might not be able to ever pay him back. But he was gone. He wouldn't listen.[6]

Floyd Bell, *publicity director of the Boston Sportsmen's Show in the early '50s:*

Ted had tremendous admiration for Jim Thorpe, who was appearing in the show that year. Ted always called Thorpe the greatest athlete of the century—an Olympic champion, an All-America football player, a major league outfielder with the New York Giants, a major league football player.

Ted found out Thorpe was down on his luck. He found out, too, that Thorpe had been admiring one of the trailers he saw at the show. So Ted took the $3,000 out of his salary and bought the trailer for Thorpe, presenting it to Jim at the conclusion of the show. Thorpe towed it home.

Just like that. No publicity. No thanks. Ted liked Thorpe, knew that Jim would love to live his remaining days in the trailer. So he bought it for him.[7]

Dario Lodigiani:

Here he was, a guy hitting .400. I asked him one time, "Hey, Ted. How about letting me have one of your bats?" You know, to touch any of his bats or to be around them was a no-no; I'm a son of a bug, I asked him for a bat. He said, "See me tomorrow."

The next day of the game, he walked over to me and he gave me one of his bats and he said, "Don't use it while you're here. Wait'll you get out of Boston."

After a ball game in Boston, somebody presented Ted Williams with a shotgun. We came out after the game and Ted was in the middle of the diamond. And he had a bunch of kids running around in the stands, chasing the pigeons. He was out there on the mound, shooting them. We stayed there and watched it.

Bob Kennedy flew with Ted during the war. Bob came back and we were all standing around, and Ted showed Bob the shotgun. It was all engraved and fancy. Bob looked at it and said, "Oh, boy. This is a beauty." And Ted gave it to him. He said, "If you like it so much, here, you can keep it."

TWO TEDS

Tim Horgan:

Remember when he broke his collarbone? They took him to Sancta Maria hospital. The Red Sox doctors used it. A guy I know was in the hospital, Jim Cleary. He was pretty sick. They gave Williams his room. They kicked Cleary out of the room.

When Ted found out about it, he raised hell. "You can't move out a man who's sick. I want him moved into the room next to me." They moved Cleary in. And all these ballplayers were visiting Ted, and anyone that came in, Ted would make sure Cleary met him. He introduced him to them.

Cleary went to check out, and he found out Ted had paid his entire bill. Cleary's father wouldn't let him, but Ted wanted to.

He was charming. He was a fascinating guy. They had a big party for Jack Fadden, the Harvard trainer and the Red Sox trainer. It was up at the Somerset Hotel, I think. Ted was invited, because they were great friends. But he did this, and he did it on purpose—he didn't show up until the last minute. Because as soon as he walked into the room, everybody left Fadden and gravitated to Ted.

But Ted was aware of that. That's why he didn't show up until the very end. He could be sensitive.

Joe McCarthy, Red Sox manager 1948–50:

I'll never forget my first year in Boston when we tied for the championship and, as you know, lost to Cleveland in the playoff game. Ted came into my office after the game and said he was very sorry that we couldn't win.

Then he added, "Joe, they didn't think we were going to get along together, but we fooled them."[8]

*Pitcher **Boo Ferriss**, Red Sox teammate:*

I was single my early years there. I was always one of the last ones to leave the clubhouse. I wasn't in any hurry. He and Doris—that was his wife at the time—he took me home with him three times or so. "Come on home with me, and we'll have Doris cook us a steak." We'd hit the house and he'd tell Doris we were there. "Get those steaks ready."

*Third baseman **Frank Malzone**, Red Sox teammate:*

I hate to say it, but he was loud. He had a way of creating a tension by being loud and by being a big man. His presence was known because he stood up above everybody else.

There's no question, when he walked into a room, everybody knew he was there.

***Johnny Orlando**, Red Sox clubhouse man and buddy to Ted Williams:*

It ain't that he don't want to be friendly. It's just that he hates front-runners. He don't like people who run up and make a big fuss over him when he's done something good. Now take me. I never shook his hand once after he hit a home run. Never once. He don't need it then. It's after he goes 0-for-5 that I talk to him. That's when he needs it, not when he's doin' good.[9]

Eddie Joost, *Red Sox teammate:*

If Ted would like you, he'd like you and he'd show it. If he didn't like you, he'd just stay away from you. He didn't bother with you. He'd just go his own way.

Chuck Stevens, *St. Louis Browns first baseman:*

He was everybody's friend. Everybody but the press, I guess. But the ballplayers all admired him for his ability. He was a free spirit, you know. You heard stories that old Ted did what old Ted wanted to do.

George Sullivan, *a Fenway Park batboy in 1949, a Boston sportswriter in the 1950s and 1960s, and Red Sox public relations director in the 1980s:*

I've never met anybody in my life who was as electric as he was. I've met some who are electric, but none to the brilliance that he was. I mean, he'd light up a funeral parlor.

He'd come in, bellowing something as often as not. Always the sports shirt. He walked that way he walked on the field. And things would begin to happen. He was incredible. He'd walk into a room and he'd say something. And somebody would say something just to get him fired up. And he'd come back and cut loose like a string of fireworks.

It was probably the first time I ever did see him. He came into the clubhouse and he cut loose, as only he could cut loose. He was a genius when it came to swearing. He was very inventive. I've heard some pretty good swearers in my life, including my tour in the Marine Corps—especially at Parris Island. I never heard anything like him. He was in more than one hall of fame.

This was when I was a young writer. It was the year they got Willie Tasby from Baltimore. He didn't know Ted, really. It was after batting practice, and the Red Sox had gone inside to have a Coke, maybe change their shirt. The bench was empty. Willie Tasby was up one end. He had his hat pulled down over his face. He was almost snoozing. I was sitting on the bench.

All of a sudden I hear, *clomp-clomp-clomp*. One of the photographers comes around from the stands and says, "Have you seen Ted?" I said he was probably in the clubhouse. He went up the runway. I think he got almost to the staircase leading up, and Williams is coming down apparently. All of a sudden, I hear Williams's booming voice coming up the chute there, from the tunnel.

"JESUS CHRIST! Are you sure he's here? I've got other things to do without posing for pictures all the time." He's giving him the usual Williams treatment.

Apparently, some Little Leaguer, if I remember right, had saved some other kid's life. Drowning or something like that. For some reason, this kid was being honored. And they were taking his picture with Ted. And Ted had agreed to it.

So here comes Ted clumping down. The photographer says, "He's up in the box seat, Ted. I'll get him."

"Well, goddamnit, get him up here."

You hear the gate twink from the box seat and here comes the photographer and this cute little kid in a Little League uniform. Talk about saucer-eyed.

Williams, when he wanted to turn it on, there's nobody like him. It's part of his magic. "Here he comes! There's the boy I've been waiting to meet! Come on down here. Hello!" The kid's knees are knocking and everything else.

Ted grabs the kid and shakes his hand. He makes a big deal out of the kid's batting average. They took the picture, and as the kid started to leave he said, "Thank you very much, Mr. Williams."

Ted says, "Well, thank YOU. You're the guy who's hitting .580."

The kid was just floating on air. His feet don't even touch the stairs.

Now the players are starting to come into the dugout. And somebody said something to set Ted off. It took nothing to set Ted off. Williams let off a string of expletives, and in the string was something extremely vile and blasphemous. I don't even want to repeat it or see it in print.

Down at the far end of the dugout, Tasby was still taking his snooze. He jumped up so hard, I think he hit his head on the ceiling. He jumped up and he comes down, pointing at Ted. He says, "Hey, man. I am NEVER going to fly in the same airplane with YOU."

I looked up and I'm pretty sure the kid heard it. I'm thinking, *Here's a guy who just did one of the greatest things I ever saw for this kid. And he did it with his heart, and went out of his way. And then he spoiled it.*

That was Ted.

Cronin gets elected to the Hall of Fame. He's about to get inducted. They have Joe Cronin Day at Fenway Park. The commissioner of baseball was there. Williams is of course playing left field. They had all these pregame ceremonies. Somebody hit a rising line drive to him. He wasn't a bad left-fielder, you know. The problem was, he had that great loping stride. He didn't look like Jesse Owens, but he was covering a lot of ground.

Ted actually took two steps toward the plate, then saw that it was over his head. So he hit the brakes and went galloping back, leaped, and made a terrific catch in front of the wall.

It was the third out of the inning, so he's got to gallop in. He's coming across the first-base line, and here it goes—this time he did spit. You could see it glistening in the lights. He snapped his head up and gave it the spit.

So I go back into the press room, and I see Cronin sitting with some visiting dignitary. I want to find out what Cronin has to say about that. I said, "Joe, did you hear about Ted?" He said, "No." We were walking together out of the press room out on the roof. I said, "He spit again."

He lashed out at me. "What do you want me to do about it? You know better than anybody else it's not the general manager that does that. It's the manager."

I said, "I've been around long enough to know it's the general manager, ultimately."

He was just so upset that Williams had done this on his night. He was very upset and angry.

*Ted in a rare moment
of appearing at ease.
He was endlessly in
search of challenges and
dares on the baseball
field and elsewhere.*

There were so many positives. He used to have a thing
with one or more of the hospitals. I have a feeling that he left
his private number with one or more of the hospitals. "If you
have a very sick child, a VERY sick child, give me a call no
matter what the time of day or night it is. And I'll get over
there if I possibly can."

Occasionally some of the writers would hear secondhand
about some of the middle-of-the-night visits. They'd come to
Ted and say, "Hey, Ted, I hear you were at such-and-such hospital at two o'clock this morning."

I remember once, I was in the Red Sox clubhouse. He
was like sputtering to himself. You could see his emotions and
he started to turn red. "Yeah . . . yeah . . . I was. You're right.
But if you ever print it, I'll never do it again. And it will be
on your ass that you were the guy who made me stop doing

these visits." That really impressed me. Williams did it the way you should do it. Not to get your name in the paper but for the basic good of the act itself.

Red Sox catcher **Matt Batts:**

One time we were coming back from St. Pete or something. I can't remember if he was driving or if I was driving.

He says, "I'm the best driver in the world."

I says, "No. I am."

Ted says, "You might be second best. But you're not the best. You use the brake too much."

Al Longo, *whose publicity office was quartered in the Hotel Somerset in Boston's Kenmore Square, also home to Ted Williams:*

He had a suite on the second floor. The rules were that no phone calls were to be put through to Ted Williams. The operator would take messages, and she'd give them to the bellman, and the bellman would take them up to the room, but not go in. He'd slip them under the door.

This particular day, a phone call came in. The message went down to the bellman, whose name was Frank Acornley. Soaking wet, he did not weigh 145 pounds. Wiry as could be. And a redhead, with a temper to match. He took the message up.

The door to the suite was open. So Frank went into the room and handed the message to Williams. Well, Ted got up and read him off like you wouldn't believe, because he wasn't supposed to come into the room. Acornley didn't say anything, but went back downstairs absolutely livid.

Later, when Williams was leaving to go over to the ballpark, Acornley was waiting for him in the garage behind the hotel where Williams kept his Caddy. Visualize this if you can: Acornley was maybe five feet, two inches, and Williams was about six feet four. Lean back and look up at the ceiling and point at the ceiling. That was Acornley letting Williams have it, with his finger almost up his nose. He called Williams everything in the book.

Of course, Williams had forgotten what he had done. He stood there, hands on hips, not a word out of his mouth, with a big grin on his face.

Acornley ended with, "Yeah, sure, and you're grinning about it, you SOB!" And with that he stormed away. Williams shrugged and went to his car.

One week later, a phone call came downstairs: "Frank Acornley, Ted Williams wants to see you up in his room—now." Acornley said, "Tell him to drop dead." But they ordered him to go up there.

With a chip on his shoulder, he walked into the room, and there was six-foot-four-inch Williams standing there.

He said, "Here, Frank."

There was a big package on the coffee table, about half the size of Acornley himself.

"I'm sorry," Ted said. "I want to apologize. I don't know what the hell I did, but I want to apologize."[10]

*Record producer **Ed Penney,** on a 1967 visit with Ted at the Ted Williams Baseball Camp:*

Although he dominated the room as he just sat back there and talked, he would also listen. He would ask questions. Just listening to him, I was aware of the fact that this was a very special person. Not just a great hitter but a very special person. Because of his intelligence and his curiosity.

I remember one thing that he said that has always stuck with me. He said that his daughter had just got married. I asked him if the fellow was a baseball player or an athlete. Ted said, "No. No. He doesn't do that. That's the trouble with them. They don't really have anything that they're excited about."

He said, "I don't care what it is. Whether you play ball, whether you're a great athlete, whether you play tiddly-winks. You've got to be excited about something. I can't understand people who don't get excited. If you don't have enthusiasm . . ."

You can picture him talking while he's saying this. He said, "If you don't have enthusiasm for something, then find something else to be enthusiastic about. But you've got to be excited about something."

That has stayed with me the rest of my life, that he felt that way. Was it Emerson who said that nothing great was ever accomplished without enthusiasm? Ted was like that. The way he spoke, the way he walked.

As a matter of fact, he talked with us without being aware of the time that had gone by. Finally, some counselor came up and said, "Mr. Williams, everybody is waiting for you." All the kids were out on the field waiting for the graduation ceremony.

He just got carried away with what he was talking about.

*First baseman **George Scott,** who was among the many Red Sox
tutored by Ted in spring training:*

A lot of people didn't know how to take him. I think a lot of
guys looked at it like he was getting on them, but I didn't
look at it that way.

I came from Mississippi. My mother and father always
taught me, when people get on you all the time, that meant
they liked you. When they didn't have nothing to say to you,
that's when you were in trouble.

I think a lot of kids got offended about Ted getting on
them so hard. Because he got on them hard. When they
didn't do what he asked them to do, he would call them
"Bush." But it was all in fun. You had to know how to take
him. He talked at the top of his voice. That's the way Ted
Williams was. He talked loud. And once he got to talking, he
had to get your attention.

I loved the guy. He's one of the two people I always
respected in the Red Sox organization, because I really felt
that they cared about me. That was Ted Williams and Tom
Yawkey. To this day, I tell people that. I never will forget those
two men.

I remember when I was a kid, I heard about the Williams
Shift. And as I got older, I learned what that shift was like.
I'd jank with Ted a lot. I'd tell him, "I don't know who the
hell played first base in the league when you were hitting, but
they wouldn't have needed to have a shift if I played first
because I would have took a lot of base hits away from you."

He used to tell me, "OOOOOOH-BOY! Wouldn't that
have been a challenge."

*First baseman **Don Mincher,** who watched Ted lose his passion as manager of the Washington Senators and Texas Rangers:*

He could be impatient. It manifested itself by the way he acted on the bench. It also manifested itself toward the end of the season in somewhat of a disinterest. I had the feeling he wished he was somewhere else. And most of the time he did wish he was somewhere else. He wished he was fishing, mostly. There came a point where he didn't want to manage anymore.

I idolized him when I was growing up. He was absolutely my favorite player. I followed everything he did. I was crazy about the man on a personal level. We'd talk for hours about different things, different parts of life. About fishing, about his time in the armed services.

He could be very, very, disinterested, or he could become very forceful. Those are the times I don't like to remember about him.

Ted put a fifteen- or twenty-minute period after a game when no one was allowed in our clubhouse—sportswriters, anyone. And it was mainly for Ted. We knew that. Because it gave him time to get out of the clubhouse before the sportswriters got there. I never saw him throw a tirade, or throw a spread, or anything like that. He was usually out of the clubhouse before any of that could happen. Especially toward the end.

*Pitcher **Dick Bosman,** who also played under Ted with Washington and with the Texas Rangers:*

I think if he had had the temperament to stay at it longer, I think that he would have become a good manager. Just because he was a bright guy and he loved the game.

We had a good year, and we had a fair year. And then we traded away a bunch of guys for Denny McLain, which was very ill-advised. His arm was bad and he was not a good citizen. Sparks flew quick between him and Ted. McLain tried to make Ted the reason why he wasn't pitching good, because Ted wouldn't pitch him on a four-day rotation. There were plenty of times when Ted would have to go take him out, and McLain would be, "The only reason you're taking me out is blah-blah-blah, this and that." There was always some kind of problem, because McLain tried to make it all Ted's fault.

That trade decimated us. We were three good players away from being a great club in '69. They ended up giving away a couple of them, so we were five good players away.

By the time we got to Texas, it didn't look like it was going to go anywhere for him. He just kind of said, "Hey, I think it's time for me to get out of here."

Legendary Indiana and Texas Tech basketball coach and friend to Ted, **Bobby Knight:**

My wife and I are going to see him. She had never met him. We got caught in a torrential downpour in Florida on our way to Hernando. So I got there about twenty minutes late.

There's a pool and a little patio outside the kitchen. We parked the car, and I came around and went in through the kitchen. Karen's behind me, looking at the beautiful sight of where he lives, up on a hill. So I walked in the kitchen.

"GODDAMN, COACH, YOU'RE TWENTY MIN-
UTES LATE! GODDAMNIT, LOOK AT THE CLOCK!
WHERE IN THE HELL HAVE YOU BEEN?" He was just
chewing my ass off.

Then Karen comes in right behind me. Right in the
middle of him chewing my ass off, he looks at her.

"Well, now honey, you come right in here and sit beside
me."

There's a guy I knew in New York named Ed Mosler. He
was very active in the U.S. Olympic movement. When I was
coaching at West Point, he used to have me come down and
sit in his box at Old-Timers Day. He told me the story of one
time he was taking Ted to the airport with him and Musial
after a dinner in Baltimore. Musial said to Ted, "Those of us
who know what you do really appreciate how you're trying to
help Jimmie Foxx along." Jimmie Foxx was living in Cleveland, almost destitute. Ted was really trying to help him.

Williams really got upset by Musial bringing this up. He
just didn't want anyone to know that he did this sort of thing.

Have you ever read that story by John Updike? The best
sports story ever written: "Kid bids fans adieu." That line in
there, that gods don't answer letters. That's one of the great
literary lines of all time.

He wouldn't bend. He wouldn't come out and tip his hat.

It was the day before, or maybe the day I was inducted into
the Basketball Hall of Fame. They had a ceremony for him at
Fenway Park. He came out and talked to the fans. We were sitting in a sports bar in the Marriott Hotel in Springfield.

When he stepped to the microphone, I told my wife, I
just knew exactly what he was going to do. I said, "You watch
this. This is going to be one of the great dramatic gestures
that you've ever seen. The son of a bitch has got a hat some-

where and he's going to pull it out and tip it to the fans." And that's just what he did.

Infielder **Johnny Pesky,** *Red Sox teammate and long-time friend:*

Early in '42, I remember having dinner with Bobby Doerr one late afternoon. Ted hadn't reported the first three or four days because he had to stay in Minnesota and get his draft thing straightened out.

Ted came in and went over to see Bobby. That's when I first met him. He and Bobby were talking, and he finally looked over at me and says, "You're the kid shortstop, huh?" I said, "Yuh." And I didn't say anything more. I let him do all the talking.

People liked to be around him because he was so . . . magnetic, I guess is the word. He was very charming. Of course, he could get mad, too. When he got mad, you'd just shut up. He had strong likes and dislikes. He stirred the pot, I'll tell you that.

When he was young, he was a cantankerous young man. But he was never a violent guy. You'd think he was violent, but he wasn't. He was a pussycat.

In 1942, we went into that navy program in July. We didn't get called until after the season. We went up to Amherst College together because we were in the same naval program. He was very bright. He took to everything fast. There wasn't anything he couldn't do, and do it well. He knew what he wanted to do, and he did it. His mind was so quick. He was a great reader, too. He read a lot. He had a high school diploma; he wasn't what you would call a highly educated guy. But as far as I was concerned, he was a Phi Beta Kappa.

John Henry [Ted's son] calls me his godfather. Not legally, but he refers to me as his godfather. I took him in when he was a little kid. He spent some time here. He's like a son. When I was coaching, he stayed here a couple of summers. He was just a kid. He was around fourteen. He spent some time with Ted in the spring.

Ted wanted to discipline him all the time. Ted thought I was kowtowing to him. He thought I was giving him spending money, and I never did. One time, he needed some money, but he was hesitant to ask me. Finally he got the courage to ask me. Maybe it was twenty-five bucks or something. I said, "I'm going to give you this money, but you've got to pay me back." By God, he paid me back. But he wouldn't tell his father about it.

Ted isn't as strong as he used to be, but his mind is good. John Henry is right with Ted. Ted loved them all. Their association became close. Now John Henry is in business with his father. And now he's down there with him. Ted needs that. And I think John Henry realizes that. We're all pleased with the way things turned out. It's just like a family.

Maureen Cronin, *daughter of Joe Cronin:*

He's my favorite subject in the whole world. I remember his coming to our house. And I remember him helping a little boy who had leukemia, who was a nephew of some neighbors of ours in Newton Centre. I remember this little boy, who must have been seven or eight, had come down with leukemia, and he was pretty much dying. Ted went to the hospital to visit him. I remember thinking what a very nice man Ted Williams was.

We have a very special relationship, because he loved my dad. I was very close to my dad. I grew up knowing Ted. We'd send Christmas cards and talk to each other. Saw each other at spring training every year. He was part of the family growing up. I remember spending a lot of time with him at the ballpark, at the Hotel Somerset where he lived, him coming to the house, and him playing a lot of golf with Dad. He was always present. I spent a lot of time at the ballpark with my dad, travel with the team and see the women waiting in line for Ted. I was always very jealous.

My mother had a very unique relationship with Ted in that she was very much his mother in a lot of ways. She would lecture him a lot. "Button your shirt up. You might catch cold. Put a jacket on. You might hurt your arm." Things like that. She was kind of treating him like a kid in the beginning. It's kind of a joke between the two of them. Mother was always very motherly toward Ted.

He's a unique individual. If you stop and think about an individual who decided he wanted to be the best hitter of all time—not that you want to make the big leagues, not that you want to make the Hall of Fame, not that you want to hit .400—he wants to be the best hitter of all time. He's taking on Babe Ruth and Ty Cobb and Honus Wagner and all the others. That's really quite a lofty goal. And here's a man who went after it and did it.

He always had a tremendous presence. Just a handsome, fabulous presence. Kind eyes. I had a terrible crush on Ted. I always assumed when I was a little girl that when I grew up, I would marry Ted. All the girls liked Ted.

Was he a charmer? My goodness, yes. He's very bright, and when he focuses in on you and you have that conversation with him, there's nothing better. He always used to call me sweetheart, which is why I thought we were going to get married when I grew up.

I remember when I was seven or eight and we were in a coffee shop together. I was climbing up on the stool and there was this woman behind the counter and she had a big red beehive hairdo and tons of makeup on. She was very dramatic, I guess is a good way of saying it.

He said to her, "I'll have some coffee, sweetheart." And my heart just sank. I thought I was his sweetheart. I've always said Ted was the first man to break my heart.

As I got older and I saw what the press was doing to him, it was very aggravating. The Ted that I knew was very kind and loving and wonderful. He was my hero. Everybody worshiped Ted Williams in those days.

Dad was probably close to being a father image and a brother image to Ted. They were very, very close. Dad being the manager, he used to try to give him counsel about the press. You know, Ted was a very sensitive person and I think the press was very hurtful.

When my dad was dying of cancer, Ted called him every day. Sometimes when you're that sick, people call you to say good-bye, but they don't call you all the time. But Ted is just wonderful when people are down and out like that.

I think if you know anyone who's in the limelight, they have to have this kind of tough veneer. People are very demanding of them. It's not that they don't want to give you some time, it's that people can be too demanding. Ted would always try to be as cordial as he could. But Ted was his own man and he liked to go and do his own thing. Sometimes people didn't understand that.

I always say that Ted needed another planet. You look at what he has accomplished. Ted Williams was one of the best fishermen, so he kind of conquered the seas. He's one of the best baseball players, so he kind of conquered the land. He was an ace pilot, so he conquered the air. So he's kind of a man who's outgrown this planet. He's the real John Wayne.

You really have to meet Ted and have a conversation with him to understand his psyche. He's very bright and he asks you very pertinent questions. He quizzes you. If he thinks that you're answering correctly, then he surmises his opinion of you. Then you're either a friend or he goes on to the next thing.

Ted did whatever he wanted to do whenever he wanted to do it. He would kind of come and go whenever he wanted. If he had a golf game or a fishing trip, he just kind of went to his own beat. He was tough to pin down. He was always a very spontaneous man. He would say, "I'll meet you at nine." Then he would go off on his own time sequence. He did what he wanted to do.

The ironic thing is, because of his health, now he's very dependent on other people. The children and everybody who is around him. He's gotten very close to a lot of people in the last ten years that he wasn't close to before, because he kind of did his own thing before.

Before, he would always be off on a fishing trip. Once he was incapacitated, and he had people calling him all the time to see how he was, then he began to realize he had to be more accessible to us. We've seen a tremendous mellowing of Ted in the last ten years. I think that's made him realize how wonderful relationships are.

TERRIBLE TED

Ted's relationship with the press was a lot like mine. I always admired him for that. He just said what he thought.
—BOBBY KNIGHT

He dubbed them the "knights of the keyboard," so of course Ted Williams would joust with them. Ted vs. the press—especially the Boston press—was one of the great battles of the twentieth century.

It was almost inevitable. They were a flammable combination.

Boston's large collection of daily newspapers competed heavily and dispatched battalions of reporters to the ballpark in search of angles. Too much close inspection could rub anything raw.

And here was Ted, a bundle of quirky angles. He was brash, impolitic, loudmouthed, argumentative, and easy to ignite.

Good copy.

And a juicy target. The newspaper boys ripped him for his draft status, bashed him for not visiting his folks in San Diego during the winter, knocked him for racking up great statistics, kicked him when his statistics slumped, boiled him for staying in Florida while his first daughter was born in Boston.

And when Ted—who said he didn't care what they wrote and then read every word—fired back and steamed over, it meant more big, black headlines.

Great copy.

Many Boston writers liked Ted, others found him unbearable. At least one made a shtick out of ripping him relentlessly—Dave Egan, also known as the Colonel, the sodden, blistering columnist for the *Boston Record*.

It was a long war, with many spectacular battles and much collateral damage, and the rubble bounced for decades.

George Sullivan, a Fenway Park batboy in 1949, remembers the proud day he returned to Fenway Park as an eager, fresh-faced sportswriter:

I went through the green door and into the Red Sox clubhouse. As fate would have it, the first guy I saw was Mel Parnell. He had always been just a prince of a guy. Very friendly when I was a batboy.

Mel jumped right up and came right over to me and gave me a great reception. After a minute or two, you could see into the training room, and Parnell yells, "Ted! Ted! Look who's here."

And Ted says, "Jee-sus Christ!" He comes out, like John Wayne. When he wants to be, he can be the most cordial guy in the world. He throws his arm around my shoulder and he's shaking my hand.

He said, "What are you doing now?"

I said, proud as punch—hell, this is my first big assignment—"Ted, I'm a sportswriter now."

It looked like I had hit him with an electric prod. He just dropped my hand and stepped back and looked me up and down with almost disdain. He said, "You used to be a good kid. Where did you go wrong?"

It sounds like a funny line—and it is—but he was serious.

Boston Braves outfielder **Max West:**

I played in high school against him and in the Coast League, so whenever we'd see one another, we'd say hello. You know, two fellows from California. I used to run into him at the old hotel in New York, the one over Grand Central Station. A few times a year, we would be coming in and the Red Sox would be in the lobby, waiting to leave.

One time, it was when he was having all that trouble in Boston. He said something in the papers about, "I don't like your trees, I don't like your streets, I don't like your river. I don't like your whatever." He was having a big, big beef. He didn't like anybody or anything about Boston.

I made a mistake. I mentioned that.

I looked around, and all the ballplayers had left. I was standing there alone with Ted, and he was screaming in this big lobby. And he didn't mince words, you know. And here I am, listening to how lousy these people and everything in Boston was.

That was the last time I asked him about that.

Long-time Boston Herald *columnist* **Tim Horgan:**

He was very difficult. I walked into the middle of this thing. Ted was mad at Dave Egan, he was mad at Harold Kaese, he was mad at everybody, I guess, except for a very few. I walked into the middle of it. I didn't know what the hell was going on. It was tough enough to break in on the beat, especially Fenway Park, without this guy screaming and yelling at you.

With Williams, he was always the center of attention. They had a game once, and Sammy White hit a home run in the tenth inning to win it. But earlier in the game, Williams had bunted. The first and only time in his career. And the headline in the paper the next day was, TED BUNTS. Not a mention of Mr. White's home run. Which prompted Mr. White to put a sign up above his locker: "No writers."

All anybody ever wanted was Williams. You go in there, and his locker was way down on the end of the dressing room. You'd circle around. Nobody ever went directly to Ted. You'd circle around and you'd chat with this guy and that guy. Then you waited for writers like Arthur Sampson or George Carens, who got along pretty good with him, to go in and break the ice. Then everybody would drift over. Then there'd be the usual mob scene.

It was funny. If he had a bad day, he was at least approachable. I wouldn't say congenial—approachable. If he had a good day—look out. He was going to give you all kinds of hell.

I think he expected a lot of himself. I think he couldn't tolerate failure. This is just a theory I had. The fact that when he had a good day, he was very difficult to deal with, and when he had a bad day, he was approachable. I don't know if that gave him humility or not. He was a tough guy to psychoanalyze.

He'd scream and yell at you. One time I ran into him— this was early in my career. Two things he would talk about were fishing and boxing. I was covering the fights at the time. Rocky Marciano was going to fight Archie Moore. Ted loved Rocky.

So I'm talking to Ted in the dugout. He says, "I'll bet you Rocky is going to kill him." I said, "Ah, the other guy is going to beat him." I'm doing this just to get a conversation going. Well, anyway, we bet five bucks. Which I cannot afford to lose. I take Moore by a decision; he takes Rocky by a knockout.

Now I'm watching the game and I'm thinking, *No way Moore is going to go fifteen rounds. He's ninety years old.* I want to change the bet after the game.

So I go down to the clubhouse. I should have realized, no one is going near Williams. He had a helluva day that day. I wasn't even watching the game. I'm worrying about my five bucks.

So nobody's going near him. But like a nut, I go right across and I said, "Ted, I'd like to . . ."

I don't remember one word of what he said, but boy, did he say it. Oh, he's screaming and yelling. I'm the rookie on the beat. The whole clubhouse is quiet. Everybody is looking at us.

I'll never forget, I'm walking out, and I go by Sammy White's locker. He looks up and he winks at me and says, "Welcome to the big leagues, kid."

George Sullivan:

Williams had to have been one of the most intelligent people I've ever known. I think he could have made his career in so many different ways. He was an exceptional photographer. If he could have kept a civil mouth, he would have been a great announcer. Not only his knowledge, but the resonance of his voice, the quality of his voice. He just was intelligent. And he knew things. Like how to get back at writers.

My first road trip was to Washington and then on to New York. The writers told me, "Look out when you hit New York. That's where he pulls his crap in New York to get you in trouble." His favorite one to get was Joe Reichler, who was the long-time AP guy, and maybe one of the other New York writers and give them some scoop. He'd get them aside and give them the scoop, not in front of everybody.

Joe would write it. So some big scoop would come rolling over the wires by Joe Reichler, Associated Press: "Ted Williams says this is his last year," or something like that. He'd give him some scoop.

The Boston writers would be woken from their sleep the next morning from all the irate Boston sports editors, saying, "What are we spending big bucks, sending you on the road for? Why can't you get stories like this?" Williams strikes again.

So, there was a case where he and Jim Piersall weren't speaking in the outfield. This was 1956. Something had happened in Baltimore. Tom Monahan was a writer for the *Boston Traveler*. Williams wasn't speaking to some of the writers, including Tom Monahan. Piersall knew it. Piersall and Williams were always at each other's throats a little bit. Often in fun, but often stronger than fun. They were behind the cage during batting practice. Williams had hit and was heading back toward the dugout. Piersall was behind the batting cage with Tom Monahan.

Piersall said something like, "Watch me get his ass." He yells, "Hey, Ted! Hey, Ted!" Ted snapped his head around. Piersall grabs Monahan with two hands to his head and he kissed him on the cheek. A big sloppy kiss on the cheek.

Williams went nuts. Well, I don't know if he went nuts, but he was very unhappy. So Williams and Piersall weren't speaking.

I heard about it on the trip. We were traveling by train in those days. On the train between Washington and New York, I tried to get Ted. He had a private compartment. I went and I knocked on the door. He didn't answer. I couldn't find him.

I said, "No sweat. I'll get him when we check into the hotel."

So we get to New York. We get to the Commodore. The traveling secretary would put keys out on a table in the lobby. I camped out there, knowing that Williams had not come over on the bus from the train station.

He did show up to get his key. So I said, "Hey, Ted, I hear you and Piersall aren't speaking."

He just blew up. "Trying to stir up some old shit, huh?"

I said, "That's not shit. It's interesting if two guys who are playing alongside each other aren't speaking."

So anyway, he starts teeing off. One thing I learned as batboy was, the only way he would respect you was, if he cursed you, double-curse him back. That was the only way that he would respect you. I used to see guys kowtow to him, writers when I was fifteen, and even then I could figure it out. I could see his reaction. If he got all over you, you couldn't just stand there and take it.

So I went back at him. We were toe to toe.

I can remember people, customers in the lobby, just putting their hands over their ears. They just couldn't believe it. We were going back and forth. And then he just bounded off.

Sullivan, for one, handled Williams just right. **Freddie Corcoran,** *Ted's long-time agent:*

I can remember once when he had come to Boston on one of those signing-of-the-new-contract affairs, and all the writers were gathered in the ballroom of the hotel waiting for him to come in. They stood around in a circle, about a dozen of them, and they took him apart. You never heard such knocking. They hated his guts, everything about him. While they were talking, Ted came in, and all of a sudden, the place went quiet. If they had just spoken up there, while he was there, you could have had some respect for them. But all anybody said was, "Well, you've finally got here, huh, kid?" If Ted overheard anything before they saw him, no wonder he held them in such contempt.[1]

Yankees infielder **Jerry Coleman:**

He was under terrible pressure there. The Colonel [Dave Egan] was all over his ass for years. The one thing about Boston that was difficult—they would have five guys from one paper covering the Red Sox. One guy wrote the game and the other guys would look for dirt. It was really a very difficult thing. He survived all of that.

I think the funniest thing I ever saw was when he hit the home run and he hit home plate and spit at the press box. I was there. We watched him circle the bases and he got about eight feet from home plate and he jumps as high as he could: *Ptooooo*.

He was really a very gentle man. He was controversial from the standpoint that he was explosive in a lot of ways.

When we were called back into the service in the spring of 1952, we had to go to Jacksonville to take our physicals. There was a little guy named Hy Hurwitz, a little tiny writer. Ted and I were in a hotel. We were meeting there down in the lobby—it was sort of a rotunda. The hotel ran from one street to the next.

So we come out of the elevator into a passageway. Here's little Hy, and Ted spotted him a half a block away. He starts yelling, "You little son of a bitch! You get the hell out of here!"

Tim Horgan:

If you could get him, he was a hell of an interview. He was very interesting, and he knew what he was talking about. He was clever. If you got a quote from the guy, you were golden. He was dynamic.

The first time I ever met him, I was with the *Traveler* and I was in the clubhouse. Nobody was there. I'm looking for a story. It was an off day.

I was sitting in the clubhouse. They had what were like picnic tables in there. I was sitting at one of the tables and I hear, *clunk-clunk-clunk*. He comes walking by with a towel around his waist, shower slippers, and he's going into the shower room. So he looks at me. He doesn't say a word. He looks at me.

He comes *clunk-clunk-clunking* back and he says, "You a writer?"

I said, "Yeah."

"What paper?"

"The *Herald-Traveler*."

He said, "Good, it's better than that f—— *Record-American*."

He goes by, then he comes back AGAIN.

"I was over at MIT today."

I said, "MIT?"

He said, "Some professor over there has figured out what makes a baseball curve." Now he goes into a big long song and dance about these laser beams.

He says, "When you come right down to it, a baseball curves the more you spin it."

I said, "Oh, then you should throw it underhand."

He said, "UNDERHAND? You throw it OVERHAND, you stupid son of a bitch. Oh, boy. WRITERS!"

Red Sox catcher **Matt Batts:**

He got a lot of bad publicity that should not have come to him. The things that he did, if he was here and now, and he did them now, no one would say a durn thing about him. I guess they thought he should bow down or something. He just wanted to play ball.

I think there were seven papers in Boston in those days, and they were always looking for a headline. I remember one real bad one was, when he was hurt in an All-Star Game, he would just keep going out and working out when they didn't want him to, because he would never get well.

So Tom Yawkey sent him to Maine or somewhere to fish for a week so he would get well. Of course, we were in the pennant deal with the Yankees. So the stories came out that Williams abandoned his team to go fishing and all that and that we were all mad about it. Well, that was absolutely nonsense.

So Ted catches a plane and comes back. He's out on the field working out. And all the press found out that he was back and they just loaded the dugout full of them. He was out in left field, shagging balls. When our practice was over, instead of coming in, he got the greenskeeper to let him out the back gate and he walked around the durn stadium and came in the other way to the clubhouse.

There were some unhappy members of the press in that dugout. That was Ted.

Tim Horgan:

He always talked to the out-of-town writers just to screw the Boston writers. You know what he'd do? He'd be in the dugout and an out-of-town writer would come in and he'd give him a big handshake. "Let's get out of here." They go down to the end of the dugout, all alone. They'd be talking, and all the Boston guys would be looking and wondering what the hell he was telling him. Maybe he was quitting or something. Ted did it on purpose.

This out-of-town writer who didn't know him came in and said, "May I have an interview, Mr. Williams?" Ted says to him, "What did I hit in 1948?" The guy says, "I don't know." Ted says, "How the hell can you talk to me when you don't know what I hit in 1948?" He's screaming at the guy. "YOU DON'T KNOW ANYTHING ABOUT ME!" He would embarrass you. You had to be very careful.

You were never afraid of him physically. There was no indication that he would ever lay a hand on anybody. The problem was his voice. He was so loud and clear. He would just dominate you. He cowered you. He'd say anything to you.

He was moody. Very moody. You'd throw your hat in the door and see if it'd come flying back out.

Ted was the center of the whole thing. Everything revolved around Ted. He would dominate the clubhouse. The clubhouse guy was Johnny Orlando. He was actually Ted's private secretary. "OR-R-LANDO!" Whatever Orlando was doing, he'd drop it and run over to Ted. He dominated the clubhouse. He dominated the club.

Eddie Costello was my first sports editor at the *Herald*. He knew Williams pretty well. Eddie didn't cover baseball per se, but he'd go to spring training and he'd go down there. He had two theories. One theory was that Williams was a moon person. Eddie would say, "You watch. When the moon is full, that's when Teddy acts up." There's some scientific proof of this, you know.

Eddie would also say, "Ted hasn't done much lately. Two weeks, and not much ink for the bastard. It's got to be coming up." And sure enough, something would come up.

The thing that antagonized him was [Dave] Egan. He just hated Egan. Egan never went to the ballpark. Ted never saw him. I don't think Ted ever met him in his life.

Ted came up to Costello one day, and there was this big dinner that night. He said, "Give me your necktie. I need your necktie." Costello said, "For what?" Ted said, "I'm going to go to that dinner tonight."

Costello said, "Why?"

"Because Egan is going to be there."

Costello said, "No. I'm not going to give you my necktie. You're just going there to raise hell."

But he was obsessed by the guy. I don't blame him. Egan ripped him something awful. But Ted liked his ink, and he knew how to get the ink.

Red Sox teammate **Eddie Joost:**

It was really a bad thing. Here's a guy who's one of the greatest players and a good guy—he was a nice person, I don't care what anybody said. I know Ted pretty well, and he's a great person. My point is, I never heard anybody ever say anything really bad about him other than the press out of Boston.

I was playing short, and a ball was hit out to left field. Ted could play that wall like no one else. There were these light covers on the lights out there. Well, Ted backed up and he saw that he wasn't going to be able to catch it, so he moved out to catch it off the wall. Well, it hit one of those covers on the lights and deflected over toward center field. It turns out they got a couple of runs out of it. I think we lost the ball game.

A writer wrote a full-page story about how Williams had lost the ball game. The writer explicitly explained how Ted didn't do this and he didn't do that. He should have gotten here and he should have reached up. He went on and on. And there were pictures that showed the ball and all this.

So we put a copy of the paper in Ted's locker. So we're sitting there laughing. Ted comes in and grabs it and he tore it all apart. "I'll tell that SOB what the hell . . ." We said, "Hey, Ted, we were just kidding around."

He said, "This guy shouldn't be writing things like that. You know what happened."

In those days, Ted used to sit with a chair against the door that led into the clubhouse. It was restricted to the press for fifteen minutes after the game. Ted would sit there with his chair against the door for fifteen minutes to make sure that nobody got in.

This one time, the next night, Ted hit a home run in the ninth inning to win the ball game. This very reporter came in. It was myself, Ted, and Jackie Jensen on the trainer's table. We were just talking back and forth. The reporters were roaming around. This one guy came over, and Ted right away said, "I'm going to kill him. I'm going to kill him." We said, "No, Ted, leave him alone."

Ted ran the guy right out of the clubhouse. It was all verbal, though. That's the way it was with Ted.

The spars and jabs might have been real and they might have been show. They were likely a combination of both. Boston Herald baseball writer **Joe Cashman:**

Once a Boston writer, who often had feuded with him, asked if he could get him four tickets for a certain game at the Fens.

Ted came up with the tickets. He had to pay for them and the writer expected to recompense.

"What do I owe you?" he asked the Kid in the clubhouse.

Ted jumped to his feet, fire in his eyes. It appeared for a moment he'd take a swing at the scribe.

"Don't insult me. When I give something, I don't expect to be paid."

A veteran baseball writer died suddenly on a western trip.

That night, Ted called the paper. He wanted to know the financial status of the deceased's family.

"I'm prepared to take care of all the funeral expenses," he said. He was thanked but told it wouldn't be necessary.

Maybe Ted was rough on writers sometimes, but he never was rough on official scorers. He never was known to complain he had been robbed of a hit, even though there were times when he actually was, in New York and Detroit in particular.

He hit a vicious line drive to deep right in a game I was scoring at Fenway. The right fielder caught the ball after a long run, couldn't slacken his speed, crashed the grandstand wall in foul territory and dropped the ball.

I ruled an error. You should have heard the roar of the crowd. I thought they might be coming up to the roof to lynch me.

I asked Ted the next day what he thought of the ruling.

"What ruling are you talking about?"

I explained.

"I heard the boos of the crowd but I didn't know what caused it all. What else could you have called it but an error? The fielder had the ball firmly in his glove and dropped it. I wouldn't want a hit on that and I'd expect an error if I dropped it."

After one bitter battle, Ted delivered an ultimatum.

"I've hit on a way to stay out of further controversies with you guys. From now on, don't any of you talk to me. If you do, it won't do you any good. I won't answer. I'll talk to no newspaperman on or off the field for the rest of the season. That goes for all, friend or foe alike. You'll only be embarrassing yourself if you speak to me because I won't even let on I hear you."

That very night, after a game, I dined with an out-of-town couple in the Polynesian Room at the Somerset. They had been at the game and long had been Williams worshipers. They had heard that he frequently went into the room for an afternoon snack since he lived in that hotel.

I knew that if he showed up this evening, my friends would like to be introduced. In view of his ultimatum of a few hours earlier, you can bet I was praying he'd not show.

But he did. We didn't see him come in. A waiter informed us he was sitting at a table far back in the room where he couldn't be seen from where we were sitting.

Well, there I was. I had to put up or shut up. I went to his table. Two ladies were dining with him.

"What brings you here? What do you want?" he said.

"I'd like you to do me a favor."

He jumped to his feet. "Where are we going?"

I told him just up to the other end of the room.

"Oh, that's easy," he said. "I thought we'd be going out of the hotel."

I introduced him to my friends. He was never more gracious and charming as he conversed with them for at least ten minutes. Then he returned to his friends.

The next day on the Sox bench, I started to thank him.

"Keep your damn mouth shut," he said in an undertone. "Don't you know I'm not talking to the press?"[2]

George Sullivan:

He spit three times. One of them was in a twinight double-header against Kansas City. He hit his four-hundreth home run. So he's going around the bases, and as he goes across the plate, he snapped his head up toward the press box and I thought he mouthed "F— you." I looked around both ends of the press box and nobody seemed to notice anything. It could be me, but it was a question I could ask him after the game. "What did he say when he crossed the plate?"

After the game, it's getting late. It was a twinight double-header, so it's like midnight when the second game gets over. He was in, getting a shower. I waited for him by his locker. He comes out, he's toweling himself off.

"What do YOU want?" With him, it was almost like a game. Some of the stuff, you knew he meant. Some of the stuff, he was just being Ted Williams.

I said, "I want to know what you said when you crossed home plate."

He said, "What do you mean?"

"Did you say f— you to the press box?"

It was funny. He broke into a grin, but he seemed to be mad at the same time.

"Yeah," he said. "I SPIT at you bastards." Everything stops. He booms with his voice. He boomed it. He didn't need a microphone. It was like a Class B western. The bad guy comes into the tavern and everything stops dead. Freezes. Well, everything in the locker room freezes when he says, "I SPIT at you bastards."

I said, "No, you didn't. I would have seen that." From the first row in the old press box, you could see everything in a guy's face. You're right on top of the action.

Now he's really ripped up. He got all red. Really red. He said, "That's right, that's right. I didn't spit. But I MEANT to spit at you bastards. All you bastards are the same."

Then he went stomping off into the trainer's room.

All the people who had been frozen on the spot become animated. And they rush me. Especially the writers. "What happened? What started that?" So I told them the whole story.

I was still sort of mad, so I waited. I left the locker room and I waited outside the locker room for him to come out. And here he comes.

I said, "Are you serious about that? Are you lumping me with everybody?" I was a sensitive kid. I was twenty-one or twenty-two.

And I'll never forget. He burst into a big smile, put his arm on my shoulder, and said, "Don't take it personally, for crissake."

It was almost like he was being fatherly with me.

The sportswriter who hurt Ted the most was wrinkly, sour Mel Webb of the Boston Globe. *On the opening day of spring training in 1947, Williams greeted the old scribe by saying, "Why don't you drop dead, you old bastard?" Webb vowed to get back at him, and he did during that season's MVP balloting: He completely left Triple Crown winner Williams off his ballot. Ted lost the award to DiMaggio, 202–201. If Webb had voted Ted at least tenth most valuable, Williams would have won.* **Bobby Knight:**

One time, this thing comes up about DiMaggio. I was on his ass about DiMaggio. I said, "Ted, let me tell you something, and I believe this very strongly. In 1947, a Boston writer doesn't vote for you in the top ten in the MVP award. And you miss it by a point. Or you miss by that guy not putting you on the ballot at all. If that guy puts you at tenth place, you're the MVP. DiMaggio accepts the award. If your positions were reversed, you never would have accepted that award."

And you know, Ted never said a word. He looked at me and just changed the subject. That was enough answer for me.

I mean the guy, in his way, is one of the classiest people I know. One of the most honest guys. He wasn't going to say, "Yeah, that's what I would have done," and put DiMaggio in that position.

He didn't say, "No, I wouldn't have," either. He just didn't answer. I thought the non-answer was one of the greatest answers he had ever given me about anything.

Tim Horgan:

Remember the time Teddy spit? I'm down at Silver Sands beach down in Milford, Connecticut, on vacation. I'm standing out in water up to my ankles, and I see this guy running across the surf in his clothes, fully dressed.

He runs up to me. Are you Mr. Horgan? I said, "Yeah."

"I've got a telegram."

I thought somebody had died. The telegram was from my boss, Arthur Siegel, telling me that Teddy spit at the fans. It happened in New York. I am to go down to Yankee Stadium, take a seat in the left-field stands, and observe Teddy. This is how important the guy was.

So George Carens—he was one of the writers who liked Ted; he was a wonderful man—but he was the only one in the world who didn't see Ted spit. The next day, he was saying, "I can't believe these RUMORS that Ted spit." I was with George the next day. He walked into the dugout and he sees Williams.

He says, "Ted, my boy . . ."

"Get out of here, you old . . . ," Ted starts screaming.

Norm Zauchin, the Red Sox first baseman, stood up and said, "Listen, this is the only guy in the world who defended you after what you did. You should treat him with more respect." He gave him hell. And Ted took it. Because he knew he was wrong.

Maureen Cronin:

So much of what the press wrote was hurtful to Ted. Dad would talk to Ted for long periods of time. He would just sit and talk to Ted. . . . He would let Ted just rant and rant and rant and rant—and Ted would. Dad would listen to him and give him some counsel. And then it would be over.

I remember one time Ted was particularly upset about something after a baseball game. He and Dad and Tom Yawkey sat down and hashed things out. Ted was very upset.

Middle age only made him grouchier. **Tim Horgan:**

His last year, in '60, he was miserable. He wasn't well. He'd come out on the hottest days with this turtleneck sweater on. He was pale. He'd walk into the dugout and sniff the air and say, "Jesus, something smells. There must be a writer around here." You couldn't approach him. The photographers would come near him and he'd say, "Jesus, you already got nine thousand pictures of me. Why do you need more?"

He wasn't happy with himself. He wasn't happy with the whole world. He had a helluva year. But that was the worst he ever was. You didn't even try to approach him.

His last game, he went after Ed Linn (of *Sport* magazine) in the clubhouse. We weren't even allowed in the clubhouse before the game. Ed Linn went in, and Ted gave him hell. Not because of Ed Linn, but because of *Sport* magazine. *Sport* magazine, maybe twenty years ago, wrote a story about Ted that Ted didn't like. He could do that. He was just irrational. He was miserable.

Then, after he hit the famous home run, we're all down in the clubhouse and he won't see us. They sneak him out of the clubhouse and they put him in a limousine and they drive out under the stands and out he goes. He wouldn't even talk to us. It was his last game. John Updike is up there writing paeans about him.

At first, retirement didn't help. Ted was inducted into the Baseball Hall of Fame in 1966, and of course the result was screaming, big, inky headlines. **Tim Horgan:**

I was with Neil Mahoney, who was then the farm director. Three or four Red Sox officials. Bobby Doerr. Henry McKenna from the *Herald* was there. We were all sitting in one little area. Just before the ceremony, Ted got up to the microphone. He didn't know it was open.

A voice shouts out, "What would Dave Egan say now?"

I swear, Ted said, "F— Dave Egan." To this day. Because everybody—Doerr, Neil Mahoney—we said, "What did he SAY?" We couldn't believe it.

So I remember after the ceremony, Larry Claflin came over. I said, "Did you hear what Ted said before the ceremony?" He said, "No, what?" So I told him. He said, "If I heard it, I wouldn't write it anyway."

Ted gave a helluva talk. I'm working for the *Traveler*. Ralphie Long is the managing editor. I called in my story, and I said, "By the way, this incident happened before the ceremony. And I'm going to tell you, because other papers may pick it up."

Ralphie Long takes it and puts it on the top of page one: TED MARS CEREMONY. Forget all about the great speech he gave and everything.

Four days later, a guy comes down and says, "Mr. Yawkey wants to see you in his office." I never met Yawkey and I didn't know where his office was. I figured I'd better go.

I'll never forget. I walk in and Yawkey is seated at a desk on the left-hand side. On the right-hand side are [Red Sox executives] Haywood Sullivan and Dick O'Connell sitting in straight-backed chairs. I walked down the middle. There was a chair and a tape recorder. It was like the electric chair.

Yawkey says, "Sit down. I want to play this for you." It's a tape of Ted before the ceremony. You hear him say, "Ahwfgh Dave Egan."

I said, "I don't know what he said. Can you play it again?"

I asked him twice to play it, and the second time, Yawkey did a standing-sit-jump. He went up in the air, I swear, eight feet. He started screaming at me. He's yelling at me. He's calling me this, that, and everything else.

Finally, I turned to Haywood and O'Connell and I said, "If he says one more word, I'm going to punch him right in the nose. I don't take that from anybody."

Finally, Yawkey dies down and he says, "I want a page-one retraction, because your story appeared on page one."

I said, "I can't promise you that. I'm still not sure I'm not right."

When we're all done, I'm walking out the door and Yawkey puts his arm around me. He says, "If this had been me, I wouldn't have said a word to you. But Ted Williams is my friend. I always try to take care of my friends. Ted wanted to speak to you about this, but I said no, let me take care of it. And we both agree that if you do what we asked you to do, you'll never hear a word about this again. From either Ted or myself."

And I never did. And I talked to Williams many times after that, and he never brought it up.

I've got to go back to the office and tell them what happened. At that time, we were carrying the Red Sox games on WHDH, which the company owned. So we ran the retraction.

To this day, I would bet 60-40 that he said it.

*Washington right-hander **Casey Cox,** on Ted's first sentimental journey back to Fenway Park as manager of the Senators in 1969:*

Ted had a fifteen-minute waiting period after the game before he let the press in. The first time he comes to Boston, after the game [*New York Daily News* columnist] Dick Young is pounding on the clubhouse door telling him to open up and Ted is yelling at him to go f[—] himself.[3]

Ted didn't really hate sportswriters any more than he really hated pitchers. New York Times *columnist* **Ira Berkow,** *in a piece written in 2000:*

I first met Williams in 1969 when he was manager of the Washington Senators. I was sitting beside him in the dugout before a spring training game in Pompano Beach, Fla., when an elderly man came down the steps. Williams said under his breath, "What's that fella's name? I knew him when I played in Minneapolis, in the minors."

I happened to have known. "Charlie Johnson," I whispered. He was a sportswriter for the *Minneapolis Star*.

"That's it! That's it!" said Williams, jumping up. "Charlie, how ya doin'?" said Williams, shaking Johnson's hand. Old Charlie Johnson glowed.[4]

TED AFIELD

I hollered over the radio to the tower,
"He's on fire and he's coming in."
—LARRY HAWKINS, FORMER U.S. MARINE FIGHTER PILOT

Ernest Hemingway stuck a Joe DiMaggio reference into his best book, but Ted Williams was the real-life Hemingway character. Ted waded into sparkling streams to hook noble fish. Ted dreamed of felling mighty elephants on the African plain. Ted moodily dodged enemy bullets in combat.

Substitute milk shakes for absinthe, and you have the complete picture: Ted Williams as Nick Adams.

Ted was an outdoorsman and an adventurer, a good old-fashioned rugged individualist. People who were there say Ted in action was like Ted everywhere else, only more so.

San Diego boyhood pal **Joe Villarino:**

He was quite a hunter and a fisherman. We used to go down to the valley. There was nothing there, then. And I used to go rabbit hunting with him.

This one day, we went hunting and we came across this rattlesnake. Ted has his .45 with him. He just shot it and marked the spot where it was. We came back later, and he just picked up that rattlesnake and wrapped it around his neck, and took it home. He was always doing things like that.

We used to sleep out in a tent in his backyard quite a bit. We used to go swimming in a lake down in there, . . . and one time there was a little boy in there and he got tangled up in some weeds or something. I guess he would have drowned, but Ted saved his life. He went over there and pulled him out.

Ted approached fishing the way he did hitting—obsessively, scientifically, and expertly. A roommate once caught him with his head underwater in a bathtub. Ted was checking to see how a new lure would look from the fish's perspective. Red Sox teammate and roommate **Charlie Wagner:**

There was an old gentleman in Cleveland who taught him how to make flies for fishing. We used to go to the old gentleman's place. This man was a tremendous fly maker. Ted would always go see him. He loved the old gentleman.

Before you know it, within a year, the old gentleman said, "Ted, you know, you're making better flies than I ever made." He was good at whatever he undertook.

In spring training, if we were at a hotel or motel, he'd fly-cast at the back of the hotel. He could fly-cast into a little inner tube that was floating in a swimming pool. He'd stand way back and he'd see if he could hit in the middle of that little inner tube. He'd throw it in there time after time. He wasn't second-class at anything.

Red Sox teammate **Mel Parnell:**

During spring training, anytime you wanted to find Ted at night, you could go out and look on one of the bridges there in Sarasota. He was on one of those bridges, fishing somewhere.

He was a master. He could tell you what the fish was doing in the water before it took your bait.

I never went with him. I've had people tell me who have gone with him that as soon as you set foot in the boat, you've committed a wrong, because he was such a perfectionist with it all. He had set ways on it, and your ways were probably different.

White Sox and Athletics infielder **Dario Lodigiani:**

One time, Joe Gordon and I were up in the Northwest. Bobby Doerr had a place there. Ted Williams was going to come up and shoot a video with Curt Gowdy. Remember when Curt Gowdy had that program, *The American Sportsman?*

The day before Curt Gowdy got there, we all went fishing. Ted was kidding me about the way I was casting. "Just look at that guy. It's enough to make you sick."

Ted's first wife was **Doris Soule.** *He took her fishing on their honeymoon:*

He's always making me cast over again. He taught me, but he has no patience with me. And I have none with him. Often, if I land a big fish, he takes it off the hook for me and throws it back in the water. Of course, he does that with his own, too. But when I get a good catch, I want it.

We have some rows that literally rock the boat. Sometimes we fight because he won't go home and it gets so dark I have to light matches so he can see to bait the hook.

Then he's always butting in when I have a bite, telling me how to haul the line in. Usually I tell him to shut up.[1]

Sportswriter **George Sullivan,** *on a scene he witnessed while covering the Red Sox in the 1950s:*

Jack Fadden was the Red Sox trainer for a number of years. He was very close to Williams. It was amazing, because he was one of the few guys who did nothing but jab away at Ted. He was just a master needler, period.

But Ted was so vulnerable to him. He took things seriously. One time, he was giving Williams the business. The upshot was, he said to Ted, "You're not even the best ballplayer." Ted says, "Whaddya mean?" Fadden says, "Can you run like DiMaggio? Can you catch the ball like DiMaggio?"

Williams says, "Awwwwright. I'm still the best hitter. But there's one thing you can't say—that I'm not the best fisherman."

Fadden said, "Yeah, come on. There's a guy who caught a thousand more fishes than you ever did."

Williams said, "Who the hell is that?"

Fadden said, "Did you ever hear the tale of the loaves and the fishes?"

When they would start to go at it, toe to toe in this needling stuff—all in good fun—guys would come in because they enjoyed it so much. They all went nuts when he said the loaves and the fishes.

Ted says, "Yeah, yeah, but you had to go back far enough to beat me, didn't you?"

During World War II, Ted turned down the chance to spend the duration playing on service baseball teams. Nick Adams wouldn't dream of rear-echelon duty. Instead, Ted set his heart on fighter pilot wings. It was typical: Fighter pilot wings were extremely hard to get. And Ted liked the idea of "being up there by myself, with nobody else to worry about." Boston Braves pitcher **Johnny Sain:**

At Amherst, we flew small airplanes—Cubs and Wacos. Those were double-winged planes. We flew off of Turners Falls airport. We would ride out there in a bus. Amherst College was a beautiful place. They just treated us great. In fact, we needed a little extra help, and we had night classes. Ted and I were about in the same boat in that we were high school graduates. They gave us extra time at night. They helped us be able to get through that.

From there, we went to the University of North Carolina, at Chapel Hill. Ted and [Johnny] Pesky were there. Amherst was more academic. When we went to Chapel Hill, it was a

After a summer of bad press and angry public reaction about his draft status, Ted enlisted in the fall of 1942 and pursued the coveted naval aviator's wings. He won them with the Marine Corps and like many superior pilots was assigned duty as a flight instructor. He was on his way to combat duty when World War II ended.

little more physical. We did it all. Wrestling, boxing. They threw us in a pool, and we had to stay afloat for an hour. Things like that.

While we were there, we had a team called the Cloudbusters. We'd play Norfolk and such on weekends, when we got a chance to play. They kind of wanted to see Ted in New York. So we got on a train and rode up there. The Yankees played Cleveland in the regular game. Then they picked a team from the Yankees and Cleveland, and they played us, the Cloudbusters. Babe Ruth managed that team against us. He pinch-hit about the fourth or fifth inning. He hit one long foul. The umpire and I walked him—they wouldn't call a strike against him. He walked and went down to first base and jumped up and clicked his heels together.

They had a muster one day. They gave you a choice of being in the marines or being in the navy.

I thought about that. I thought, *The navy is the bigger outfit. If I'm going to war, I want to be with the bigger outfit.* I joined the navy; Ted joined the marines. After they dropped the big bomb, we got out. I was able to get completely out of the reserves because the navy had so many pilots.

Ted couldn't get out because he was in the marines. And he had to go back during Korea, and he almost got killed.

When World War II ended, Ted was in Hawaii, on his way to combat in the China-Burma-India theater. Seven years later, he got another chance. Early in the 1952 season, Ted was called out of the reserves to serve in the Korean War. He was thirty-three years old, married with a young daughter. He suspected he was summoned because of the public relations value of yanking the famous Teddy Ballgame out of civilian life like so many other regular Joes. He hated the idea of being used like that. But he went, flew thirty-nine missions in F-9 Panther jets, and picked operation commander John Glenn's brain about piloting the same way he picked Rogers Hornsby's brain about hitting. And he still found time to be Ted. Marine fighter pilot **Edro Buchser:**

By the time Ted got there, I was about finished with my missions. After I finished, they made me the provost marshal, which is the sheriff.

I had met Ted while I was flying. But then when I got to be the provost marshal, he and I were kindred souls in the hunting and fishing business. I had a fairly private office. Ted, he did not like people kowtowing to him. With Ted, what you see is what you get. He used to come down to my office because nobody would bother him there. Then we'd go duck hunting together.

We would go out and if we only got seventy-five ducks—and these were all mallards—it wasn't a good day. The reason we were so successful was because I was the provost marshal and I had roving patrols out. And one of the things the roving patrols did was radio back where the ducks were.

We hunted a lot. We used to shoot over a hundred mallards a day. We were both good shots, but he was a much better shot than I was. With a shotgun.

This fellow, Woody Woodbury, is a nightclub entertainer, and he's an old buddy of mine. He knew Ted. Anyway, Woody is after me to go duck hunting. He was an entertainer for crissake, you know?

I had two shotguns. I loaned him one. We go out. You know nightclub people—they have a lot of ego and they like to talk. Ted got so goddamn mad at Woody. He said, "Watch it, you're going to shoot yourself in the foot. Or me." Woody didn't know how to handle a gun too well.

So after we had been hunting, we're walking back just before dark. We'd only gotten like twelve ducks or something. Because Woody was always jumping around and making noise.

I was on one side of Woody and Ted was on the other. I looked at Ted, and Ted looked at me, and we both kind of puckered up our mouths and rolled our eyes. I grabbed Woody's hat—that old Marine Corps fatigue hat made out of cloth. The best hat I ever had.

I threw it up in the air and Ted fires, and Ted Williams shredded that hat. All that come down was part of the bill.

Woody looks and says, "What did you do that for?" I said, "I just wanted to see if old Ted Williams could hit that thing."

Another time, we had a general named McGee. Most generals are assholes, but he was a real good guy. I got a call from the general's aide. The general asked if he could go with me on a duck hunt. I was only a major. Sure he could go.

Well, when Ted found out about it, he didn't like that at all: "Goddamn rank . . ." Ted was really an enlisted man's officer. So the aide turns out to be an Ivy Leaguer from Harvard or somewhere. So the general met us, and we get out to where we were going to shoot ducks, and I put the general on one end of this pond—this rice paddy—and Ted was next to him, about two hundred yards upwind. I took the least likely spot, all the way upwind. So I was about four hundred yards from the general.

We're sitting there for a little bit, and all of a sudden this big flock of ducks came circling. This dumb son-of-a-bitch aide, probably never been off the hard surfaces in his life, stood up and pointed and shouted, "There they are, General!" Of course, the ducks hightailed it out of there.

I hear from Ted's blind, I can hear him grumbling. I don't know what he's saying, but I can hear the noise.

Then it happens again! This aide jumps up and points. "There they are again, General!" Of course, the ducks flew away.

Ted stood up and jacked a shell and he pointed his shotgun and said, "You son of a bitch, if you do that one more time, I'm going to blow your head off!"

But that was Ted Williams, boy. He didn't give a damn if you were the president or the colonel or what.

He valued the common man. And honesty. That's what he valued.

Ted didn't hardly have a minute where there wasn't someone wanting to come up and talk with him. When he'd go on R&R, there were the damn reporters. There was one in particular, a sportswriter that Ted didn't like at all. This guy came around the K-3 while Ted was getting ready to fly a mission the next morning. Early. Something like a six-thirty mission. He came around two o'clock in the morning and woke him up for an interview. And boy, Ted threw his ass out of that tent. I didn't see this, but I know the guys in his tent. Can you imagine? That's what he was faced with in those days.

Rank would like to be around him. I remember one time, he went on R&R for five days, and he just disappeared. No one knew where the hell he was. I think he just hopped on a train and went way outside of Tokyo. He was just looking for some privacy, that's all.

Ted was not impressed with wealth. He was not impressed with rank or society. He never wore a tie. He was very outspoken. Like, we had a colonel. He was a good colonel. I worked for this colonel. He said, "Buck, you and Ted have dinner with me at my table?" Okay. The colonel was a good guy.

But Ted and the colonel got to talking, and Ted got mad. Not at the colonel, but at the structure—the MiGs, the North Korean and the Chinese aircraft, could come across the border going south, but we couldn't go across the border north after them. And we weren't allowed to fly over where the peace talks were going on. We got into that, and Ted got so mad, he was yelling at the colonel. I'm trying to get Ted to shut up. After all, the guy was a bird colonel.

Ted really loved the enlisted men more than the officers. Ted had to be around the officers, because he was one. They always wanted to be around him. But Ted would get a baseball bat and a softball. Once or twice a week in the afternoon, he'd just go down there and hit fungoes to the enlisted men. They enjoyed it. And believe it or not, they didn't hang on him the way a lot of other people did. They were real people. He liked real people.

I had my own jeep at the time. Remember, this was a softball field. Right on the first-base line, on the outfield, where the road went, I was a couple of hundred feet away from home plate. Ted was hitting them, and they were having a good time. He saw my jeep and recognized me. He yelled, "Hey, Bush." And he hit a softball out of his hand, and if I hadn't had the jeep's engine running and jerked it into gear, he would have got me right between the eyes with that ball. It hit the back of the jeep.

He valued honesty. Boy, we used to have some great times out in the jeep, running around looking for ducks. The guy was really down to earth. For example, I was driving over in my duties as a provost marshal. I had to go over to another airfield, twenty-something miles away. Ted asked if he could go.

I was driving fast. I liked to drive fast. A bumpy road, you know? I'm going about fifty or sixty, and he's saying, "Slow down. Slow down." I just didn't say anything. I just kept driving. Finally he says, "Goddamnit, Buck, slow down!" I said, "Listen, Ted, I'm driving this frigging jeep. It's my jeep. So just shut up."

He respected that. The fact that you would present your own opinion. He respected that.

Ted introduced me to photography. He was an excellent amateur photographer. Sometimes he'd come down and we'd jump in my jeep. We'd take pictures.

You know what a papa-san was? They were these old guys, and they'd have this pack on their back that sometimes would look like it was twenty feet high. Ted and I were out together and we see a papa-san. We're taking pictures. Ted wanted to put that guy's stack of firewood on his back.

The little old papa-san, he couldn't speak English. He's trying to help Ted get that thing on him. Ted tried to stand up, and he turned himself over.

Marine fighter pilot **Tom Ross:**

We were in the same air group at K-3 in Korea. I first met him right around Thanksgiving time in 1952. He had just arrived a couple of weeks before I did. He was quite friendly with a guy named Edro Buchser, who was my shack-mate. They did a lot of hunting together. They ended up spending a lot of time in my little tin shack. I'd listen to them talk a lot, mostly about hunting.

One of the fondest memories I had of Ted was several times we had early morning missions. So we took off before light. The idea was to catch the Chinese right at first light, when they were just waking up. We'd usually leave on such missions without any breakfast. When we got back, we'd all go to the mess hall to have breakfast. There would usually be about eight of us pilots. Ted would frequently if not always talk about baseball. He loved to talk about baseball. He had everybody mesmerized.

He carried himself very well. Everybody who knew him and flew with him respected him. Even though we felt that personally he got the shaft, he was doing his job. We really didn't need him. He did his service in World War II. Somebody in headquarters was just anxious for a little publicity to get Ted Williams back on active duty. He was at a disadvantage there, because most of us there were regular officers and we had been flying constantly while Ted was off playing baseball. So he was at a little bit of a disadvantage as far as his pilot skills were concerned.

I recall a very close friend of mine, Bill McGraw, was on a two-plane mission with Ted. Bill was the flight leader. They were on their return to home field to K-3. The weather had closed in, and they had to make an instrument letdown. Ted asked if he could take the lead and do it. Ted's flying instrument ability, while he had the basic skills, he didn't have a whole lot of practice. Bill said, "Sure." He passed the lead to Ted to let down through the clouds. Bill said that Ted did pretty well on it. A couple of times, he got a little too steep in his turn, he let his nose drop and he was descending too fast. Bill said, "Pick your nose up a little, Ted. Level off a little more, slow your rate of descent a little bit." And Ted responded beautifully.

That's a demonstration that Ted wasn't there just going through the motions. He was interested in doing what he was supposed to be doing to the best of his capabilities.

Before he shipped out to the war, Ted told friends that he had a premonition that he would be killed. He was nearly right. Marine fighter pilot **Woody Woodbury:**

I remember Ted was hot, I was hot, we were all hot, because after one max-effort, they rushed us all into debriefing. We had been up there more than two and a half hours. That's a long time to sit with people shooting at you. Then we get back, and we were famished. Somehow, they didn't get the word that we were to be fed when we got back. So we had to refuel and then we had to fly back to K-3, which was another half-hour, forty-five minutes. Then we had to debrief over at K-3. It was after dark when we got back to K-3 on the sixteenth, and everybody was ticked off because we didn't have anything to eat.

I remember Ted Williams coming out of the debriefing saying, "I AM STARVING!"

They told him there was nothing to eat. He could get a candy bar.

I was with him on that mission. It was February 16, 1953. It was a "max-effort." That was a phrase used in those days. We worked in cooperation with the air force and with carrier-based navy planes. The targets were right up near the Manchurian border.

The enemy had been building bridges as fast as we were knocking them out. The powers that be decided that it would be a max-effort to knock them out with delayed fuses and all that kind of stuff.

We went over to the air force base across the Korean peninsula, on the west coast on the peninsula. We went over there on the thirteenth. We had max-effort on the fourteenth, the fifteenth, and the sixteenth.

Marine fighter pilot **Larry Hawkins:**

It was a mass strike between VMF-115 and VMF-311, which Ted and I were in. I was one of the old-timers by then. I was only twenty-two years old, but I had somewhere between forty and sixty missions. By this time, I was a pretty savvy kid.

Ted was the wingman of a division leader. He went and dove on the target. I don't remember seeing him go into the target area. But as I was in my dive, I noticed this aircraft in front of me looked like he had been hit.

He pulled up, and he started going north. I start seeing what I thought to be hydraulic fluid. Then I thought, *I better follow this guy*. Because he's going north, and our evasion route was to go out to the west, to the Yellow Sea.

Anyway, I figure I better catch up with him, because he's going north and something's wrong. I figured he might be one of our newer people—which he was. He was going in the wrong direction. You don't go north into North Korea.

I joined up on him. I looked over at him and he gave me some hand signals. I didn't know exactly what he was trying to tell me, other than the fact that he was having a lot of trouble and he didn't have any radio at this time. I closed in on him and I went underneath his belly and went to the other side of the aircraft from right to left and back again. He was still streaming this fluid.

At that point in time, I still figured it was hydraulic fluid. So I patted my head and took the lead, and I turned him to the west, toward the sea. So he joined up on my left wing.

We flew maybe five minutes, climbing all the time. The fluid kept streaming. Then I figure, "That isn't hydraulic fluid, because it would be all gone by now." Then it dawned on me: *It's probably fuel*. Knowing the Panther—I knew the aircraft pretty well—I knew that if I slowed down, the fuel would pool in the bottom of an engine chamber. It would start pooling underneath the engine, and if I slowed down, it would catch on fire.

I kept him at 250-plus knots, climbing until we got somewhere between eighteen and twenty thousand feet. By this time, we're out over the sea. I start turning south and start flying along the coastline. I kept giving him hand signals, checking with him.

We kept flying to the south, and we came to a little bay area where Inchon and that area was west of Seoul. I turned him toward one of the Seoul air force bases because it was the nearest one that I could find that was a friendly airfield. I started slightly letting down, and in the meantime I'm calling the tower to let them know I had a chick that was in trouble with no radio and I was bringing him in.

Woody Woodbury:

They landed all of us ahead of him. Larry Hawkins was the guy who led him back. Ted had no hydraulic pressure. He had fuel leakage all over. Every time he'd get into heavy air, the plane would burst into flames. Larry would make him go back up with hand signals.

We knew right away he was in trouble. We knew his plane number. Ted was one of us. He was a special person to the baseball world, but to us he was just one of the guys. When the word got out, somebody said, "Hey, that's Ted's plane." We had to maintain strict radio silence. The Koreans or the Chinese were intercepting every radio transmission. But the word got out. It didn't take long to ripple through the squadron.

As soon as we landed, the air force and these jeeps had great big signs. In great big letters, it said, "Follow me." We followed that jeep. I knew what was going on. I knew that Ted was not going to eject. He was going to bring it in.

I taxied down the live runway and signaled to my follow-me jeep that there was something wrong with my aircraft and I was going to pull off to the side. I wanted to watch this with a grandstand view.

Larry Hawkins:

He could have ejected. But he was a very big fellow. I remember seeing them put him in the aircraft down at the field at K-3. They would have to squeeze him down and pull the chute harness up over his shoulders. I'm sure he flew with his seat all the way down. With his helmet on, he was darn near the minimum clearance allowable to be able to even sit in a cockpit of that size. Ejection probably would have been a major problem for him.

I think somewhere along the line, a lot of us were reluctant to eject. Ejection seats in those days were pretty much still a trial. They were just beginning to get a good ejection seat. Friends of mine who had ejected during that period had come out with broken backs. Remember, this was the early days of jets.

I started letting down around the airfield, letting down around seventy-five hundred feet. In the old Panther, that's the height you wanted to be at around the airfield, in case you had a flameout. I did that because he had to be low on fuel. He indicated that. He had been streaming this fuel for maybe twenty minutes.

As we started slowing down into this flameout pattern, you're supposed to drop your gear and start putting your flaps down and then make your 360-degree spiral down to the field and make a landing. I gave him the gear signal—which is a crank signal with your hand. Well, the minute he reached up, he dropped his gear, the wheel-well doors came down—and he broke on fire. That was because of the slowing down and that fuel had started pooling.

He must have heard that bump or thump or whatever at that point, because he slapped his gear back up. Which surprised me, because I had started putting my flaps back down. He started drifting away from me. He wrapped it up as tight as he could get it, and he went diving toward the field. He made a tight, screaming spiral toward the field. By this time I knew that he knew that something had gone wrong.

I hollered over the radio to the tower, "He's on fire and he's coming in."

I'm trying to catch back up to him. I finally caught just about back up to him, and he came up just to the end of the runway. He was doing about 200 knots and touched down right near the end and kept on skidding. I still had my wheels and my flaps down, so I was flying about 135 knots. He kept skidding about two-thirds of the way down the runway and off to the left side. By the time I got to the end of the runway, I was looking back over my left shoulder. I could see that the body had jumped out of the cockpit and run away from the aircraft.

I didn't know it was Ted Williams until a little while later, when they cleared off the strip and cleared us into landing. I had to land there because I was running out of fuel myself.

I don't think it burned that much, even though I've read that some people saw it burn to a crisp. I don't think he had hardly any fuel left.

*Called up by the
Marines in 1952 to fly
fighter jets in Korea,
Ted told friends that he
did not expect to
survive the war. He
was nearly correct.*

Edro Buchser:

Ted used to shake his head: "I'll never jump out of that damn airplane." I don't want to use the word *afraid*. But he was not going to bail out. It was the fact that he was jumping out of his security blanket. He just wouldn't do it. And he didn't.

He was hit. He was on fire. He should have buttoned out right then. Because the son of a bitch is liable to blow up on you.

One thing he did tell me, and we were laughing about it. About six of us were sitting around. I said, "Hey, Theodore. How fast were you going when you passed over the end of the runway?"

Normally you'd cross over at 120 knots. He said, "Shit, I don't know. The last time I looked, I was going 240 knots."

So he put it down on the end of the runway and he slid ninety-eight hundred feet and came to a stop due just to pure friction on the bottom of the airplane. The only thing that stopped him from being burned at all was he came to a stop with the nose maybe twenty yards from a big, old fire truck.

Woody Woodbury:

So I pulled off the taxiway and went up the finger strip and whipped around and watched Ted as he came over the fence. He couldn't get his wheels down. He couldn't get his flaps down. He couldn't get his speed brakes down. He was really smoking badly. He slid up to probably within two hundred yards of where I was sitting. Man, that was something to see. What a melee of sparks, fire, and debris. Everything was just flying up in the air behind him.

He made a magnificent landing. He had to come in well over two hundred miles per hour. He didn't have anything to slow him down. He didn't hit; he glided in. There was no bouncing. He skidded almost the entire ten thousand feet, because he was going so fast.

His airplane sort of veered over to where I was sitting. I sat there and I couldn't believe it. Just before he came to a stop, the right wing—just like a little wounded bird—the right wing flopped over and hit. I'll tell you this: He had already jettisoned his canopy. He came out of that cockpit a lot faster than he ever ran around those American League bases. You can bet on that.

I happened to ride with Ted on a transport plane a few days after this. I remember him telling me, you know in Ted's great language, "Here, I almost busted my ass over there and I'm scared to death that airplane might blow up and I'm sort of half-running away from it, and this goddamn air force lieutenant colonel came up and asked if he could have my autograph!" That's a true story.

I'll tell you what. Ted got up the next day at K-3 and flew. You're supposed to be grounded seventy-two hours after any kind of mishap like that. Ted had a lot of balls. He got up and flew the next day. His colonel, Art Moran, got called on the carpet. Art told me later that the general really chewed him out for letting Ted go up the next day.

Ted was red, white, and blue. All this talk about him being reluctant to go in, I don't know where that ever came from. Probably from that damned sportswriter up in Boston.

Tom Ross:

I was shot down in April of '53 and I had to make a crash landing. I was too low when I was hit to eject. I put my bird down on a gravel strip and ended up with a very severe case of whiplash. I ended up on a hospital ship in Inchon with my head in traction. Ted happened to be there. He was sent up there by our squadron flight surgeon because he had a very, very bad case of sinus problems. Of course, he couldn't fly with an infected sinus.

I chatted with him briefly. I remember saying something to the effect that "I hope they're going to send you home now, Ted." He said, "I think so. I'm ready to go, too."

Larry Hawkins:

We didn't talk too much about that day. The only time we did much of that was the first time they invited me to the Hitters Hall of Fame over in Hernando. Ted introduced me to his son, John Henry, and he said, "This is the young fellow who saved my ass over in North Korea."

He was in a lot of danger. Had that aircraft broken on fire, he would have been gone. Or, if someone had not seen him going north, he would have been in bad shape up there in North Korea. He lost his hydraulics, but he must have had just enough to get himself out of his high-speed dive.

There's a good possibility he wouldn't be with us today. His daughter Claudia, after I told her the story—I became the angel to the family. Because I had saved her dad's life.

He wrote a beautiful letter to my dad. He complimented my dad for having a fine son and all that. He was very good that way. All that stuff about him being a tough guy to handle. Well, we joked around with him. We used to call him "Bush." He was a nice person. They say he might have been a spoiled star in some ways, but as a combat pilot in the squadron, he was a real nice guy.

Long-time friend **Frank Cushing:**

Of all the things Ted told me, he said, "I've gotten all kinds of accolades in the baseball department, but the thing I'm most proud of was I was a good marine fighter pilot." He was so darned proud of being a marine.

Ted Williams stalked his prey in streams and rivers, in the air, on the plains, and in baseball parks smack in the middle of a city.
George Sullivan, *Fenway Park batboy in 1949:*

This was on an off day, on a Monday. I remember coming to the ballpark. I was walking down what was then Jersey Street, now Yawkey Way, and when the Red Sox weren't playing, that was a pretty quiet street. It was around two o'clock in the afternoon. And I hear a loud bang. I thought it was a car backfiring. I looked around. There was no car or truck. I shrugged and continued walking down Jersey Street.

As I was approaching the door, I heard it again. I turned around and didn't see anything.

I made the turn and I hear the bang again. Now it's really echoing underneath the stands of an empty Fenway Park on an off day. I said, "Geez, what's going on? That sounds like it's coming from out on the field."

So I walked down toward the Red Sox clubhouse, but I took the first exit out on the field, up that ramp, and it was the damnedest sight I'd ever seen. There were dozens of dead pigeons all over the field. And I'm looking around to see what killed the pigeons. I see out in the visiting team bullpen in right field, there's somebody in civilian clothes sitting out there. I squint and I see he's got a rifle in his hands. I look even closer and see it's Ted. And he's picking off pigeons out there. It was sort of a public service. They were always the bane of

Fenway Park. Back in the '40s, it was a real problem. Pigeons used to roost under the eaves and just dump on the patrons.

I don't know if I had ever seen a weapon before. I watch for two or three minutes, watch Williams. A couple of birds would fly out from beneath the roof and—BANG! BANG!—they would go down. He had gotten in trouble for that. One of the animal rights groups complained about it, and supposedly Williams wasn't doing it anymore. Well, he was doing it.

I watched in amazement for a while. But I had jobs to do. Shoes to shine and all that type of stuff. I headed into the clubhouse. About twenty minutes later, I hear *clomp-clomp-clomp* coming up the runway from the field. Ted came up to me from behind.

"Hey, old buddy," he says.

Oh, man. When he called, "Hey, old buddy"—look out.

"Do me a favor, will ya? Get a couple of those plastic barrels and get some of those pigeons."

I went out there and I must have filled up four or five barrels of dead pigeons. And every one I picked up, holding it at arm's length, I said a new swearword.

Long-time Boston Herald *columnist* **Tim Horgan:**

I'm at the ballpark on an off day, looking for a story. Hy Hurwitz was with me. He was about five feet tall. A little guy. Williams says to him one day, "If you were fifty pounds heavier and one foot taller, I'd punch you right in the nose." Hy looked at him and says, "If I were fifty pounds heavier and a foot taller, you wouldn't dare." He looked him right in the eye.

So anyway, we're up at the ballpark. Nobody around. In those days, we used to come through the offices on Jersey Street and into the left-field stands. So we just come out of the offices and we hear, *BANG! BANG! BANG!*

What the hell is that? Ted is out in right field with Billy Goodman. There must have been hundreds of pigeons out there. Goodman would shoo them, waving his arms. They'd go up in the air and *BANG*—Ted would shoot them.

I couldn't believe this. There were dead pigeons all over the place. Hy says, "Holy geez, what are we going to do?" I said, "Number one, we're going to get down. He's liable to shoot us."

So I called Arthur Siegel, my boss. Arthur says, "I'll handle this." He called the Society for the Prevention of Cruelty to Animals. They sent a van up and they apprehended Williams. They fined him.

I had to write the story. In those days, you could refuse a byline. I said, "Don't you dare put my name on this story. I'll sue you if you do." And they didn't. I still had to deal with the guy.

For better or worse, Ted was never more himself than on a fishing trip. **Bobby Doerr:**

He was a different type person. He was a perfectionist. I fish a lot. If I make a mistake, if I get a backlash, it was no big deal. But he wanted everything to be perfect.

We went down to this place on the tip of Florida to go tarpon fishing. It's the ultimate of everything.

He took me out to these flats, where you'd see these big tarpon breaking. The night before, he wanted me to try out reels, whether I wanted a spinning reel or a level-wind. I never had used a spinning reel too much, so I said I'd like to use a casting reel—a level-wind reel. I worked on that that evening, casting and adjusting so I wouldn't get a backlash. My gosh, we go on these flats and these tarpon are breaking like porpoises out on the flat. Ted poled the boat up front.

When I got ready to cast this little lure out, I knew darn well the thing was too loose. I couldn't figure it out. I thought I had it right the night before. So I said, "Ted, this thing is too loose." He said, "No, no, no."

Three fish were rolling out right in front of me. I casted right into them and about an eighty-pound tarpon hit it. Got about fifteen feet and—*bang*—a backlash and it broke off. And he said, "WHAT IN THE . . ." I mean, the language.

So he's repairing and putting another lure on and he's cussing the whole time. So I'm standing on a little fishing box. . . . It's on the seat. That wasn't the most comfortable thing to be standing on and trying to cast off. He's poling, and all of a sudden you see this big thing laying out to the right of the boat. This fish looked like a big log laying out there.

I cast to it. It was a little awkward to be casting to the right off that box. I cast about five feet in front of the fish and spooked it. "WELL WHAT THE . . ." The language on that. He was a little riled up there.

A little while later, well, here's another one. Back over to the left, which was more of an easy cast. I made a beautiful cast, only it was at the tail end of the fish. So I spooked that off. Well, now Ted is really getting kind of disrupted and the language is getting stronger all the time. It's getting a little bit rough.

We're poling along there, and I'm standing on this box for about an hour and I go to get back down in the boat. He says, "What are you doing?" I said, "Geez, my back's getting tired." He says, "Get back up there! We're getting some fish."

I get back up on the box. In a little while, a big tarpon jumps in front of us. It must have been a 140-, 150-pound tarpon. I'm thinking, *I hope I don't see him again.* I'd had about enough fishing. I'm getting pretty shook up.

Well, sure enough, here this thing is, in front of us about thirty or forty feet. I made a perfect cast right in front of him. You could see the fish start to move toward the lure. Ted said, "Give it a little twitch." I gave it a little twitch. I had never fished tarpon before.

This thing hit and jumped about seven or eight feet up in the air. He jumped and jumped and kind of started around to the right. He must have gone sixty or seventy feet and the line broke. Ted says, "WELL WHAT THE . . ." The language is getting ten times stronger than it was.

We didn't fish much more that day, because it was getting late and the fish were getting kind of scattered out.

He was really, I mean . . . well, he admits it. He said, "I gave you a hard time, didn't I?" I said, "You surely did."

Legendary Indiana and Texas Tech basketball coach **Bobby Knight:**

He was my favorite player when I was a kid. I went to Cleveland Stadium, his last at bat in Cleveland Stadium; bases loaded in the ninth, one out, they bring him up to pinch-hit. They walk him on four pitches. He's forty-two years old, and Cleveland wouldn't take a chance on pitching to him.

The first time I ever talked to him, the secretary came in and said, "Ted Williams is on the phone." And I said to myself, "Who's this asshole calling up and saying he's Ted Williams?" So I said, "HELL-o," like that. Immediately, I hear, "All right, Coach, what size tippet do you use when you're fishing for those brown trout in Montana . . ." And I knew right then that I got the original article on the phone.

We became pretty good friends. In '91, we went to Russia. A friend of mine called me one day and told me that he had really had a great fishing trip to Russia for Atlantic salmon. As you know, that's one of Ted's three fish.

I called Ted right away. I said, "Hey, you want to go to Russia fishing for Atlantic salmon?"

"Well, goddamn, Coach, are you going to go?"

I said, "Yeah, that's why I'm calling." He said, "Well, then I'll go." That's all there was to it. He never wavered.

Before we went, Bush Sr. took him to the All-Star Game in Toronto on *Air Force One*. So he asked him, "Ted, what are you going to do after the rest of the summer?" He said, "Coach Knight and I are going to go to Russia." All Bush said was, he looked at him, and said, "You and Coach Knight in Russia. Jesus." That's all he said.

That's when his friend Louise was living with him. So I worked out a lot of things with her. I'd take Tang and stuff and make sure that he ate well and everything.

Curt Gowdy had told that you have to really watch that he doesn't get on top of you. You got to argue with him. You've got to get on his ass. He said, "Now, I know that will be hard for you, because you've idolized him. But you just can't let him have his way with you. He'll drive you nuts. You've got to get on him."

Now, we're on the plane going to Finland. We're going to Helsinki. "Okay, Coach, goddamnit, we're going to play a little GAME here. We're going to discuss the five greatest Americans of our lifetime." I said, "Well, goddamnit, look how much older you are. You got almost twenty-five years on me. That isn't fair. You've got more resources than I do."

"All right, goddamnit. Since 1900. This century. We'll talk about the greatest Americans."

Well, I know he's an arch-Republican, to the right of Attila the Hun. I said, "I'll start it off. And it's absolutely indisputable, and you can't even argue the fact, that we got to start with Roosevelt. And I'm talking about FDR. How can we start this discussion without putting Roosevelt on a pedestal that no one else can reach?" Well, that just starts it.

I mean, it was great. I mentioned Martin Luther King. He didn't disagree with that. But he said, "Now we've got to think about Joe Louis." He had a long explanation of Joe Louis being the first prominent black, and blacks listening to Joe Louis fight every time he fought. It was really good. It was a very eloquent pronouncement for Joe Louis. We went back and forth with Roosevelt and George Marshall and [Douglas] MacArthur. I needled his ass a little bit, too. I said, "MacArthur? What about [Chester A.] Nimitz? He ran the war in the Pacific." Ted was obviously very well read. And can argue like hell. He's a great debater.

I never had a more enjoyable week. Some guy asked him, "Who were the best pitchers?" He said, "Virgil Trucks and Bob Feller." I said, "Goddamn, you batted .500 or something against Bob Feller. Sure you think he's one of the best." He said, "Ah, goddamnit . . . , that doesn't make any difference."

He'd be casting, and I'd start singing the marine hymn. And he'd come to attention. We had a great time.

The first day, he says, "Okay, Coach, I've got to look at your rods. Get out your rods." So he takes my rods. "GOD-DAMN, Coach, this is pretty GOOD. Pretty GOOD, Coach. Who the hell gave you this? This is pretty good.

"Okay, the reels. Let me see . . . What a chickenshit collection of junk this is! How the hell are you going to catch these fish with this crap?" It was great. It was the best.

The first night, neither one of us had caught anything. We're sitting at the table, eating. "Well, GODDAMN, Coach, you're not BAD! I've got five days to work with you! Son of a BITCH, I'll make a fisherman out of you. DAMN, Coach, you've got some talent. That surprises me."

We caught a lot of fish. He told me if we each caught one fish a day, it would be great. I hooked thirty and he hooked twenty-two. I fished a lot more than he did. Hell, he was seventy-four years old.

We're on the plane. We're in the last row of first class. There are three seats, and I'm sitting on the right. Ted's in the middle. And there's a professor from Brandeis on his left. I'm in and out of sleep. My head is turned away from him. I'm about half-asleep.

I hear the professor say, "Ted, what's Coach Knight like?" Ted thinks for a second and he says, "Well, I'll tell you. The son of a bitch is just like me."

That's the nicest thing that anyone has ever said about me.

TED'S OPINION

*That's how I feel about it. You can print the
whole rotten mess, just as I said it.*
—TED WILLIAMS, POPPING OFF IN 1940

Getting him to talk was sometimes like storming an enemy pillbox, but often it was worth the risk. Ted Williams always had something to say, and he was worth listening to.

Ted featured a million or so opinions, always strong, often well-researched.

Documented story: In the spring of 1939, a group of Red Sox was quizzing Moe Berg about the prospects of war in Europe. Berg was a Red Sox catcher and an alumnus of three universities, a linguist, a mathematician, and a lawyer.

Ted Williams, eighteen-year-old high school graduate, burst into the conversation and blurted, "Germany and Russia will go in together if there's any fighting."

Berg quietly and patiently assured young Ted that he was dead wrong and completely misinformed.

Five months later, the Germans and Russians joined up and then World War II started.

Following is a sampling of other Ted opinions through the years.

His opinion of himself as a young ballplayer:

I never honestly thought I'd be a big league player until I played in the Coast League. I signed a contract to play for San Diego before I had my high school graduation. That was 1936. The first time I really felt I could make the major leagues was when I came up for spring training with the Red Sox in 1938. They farmed me out to Minneapolis that year for seasoning. But when I saw the fellows play at spring training camp I felt they weren't so far ahead of me.[1]

His opinion, as a young man, of the Red Sox:

When I first heard the news that I had been sold to Boston, I almost blew a fuse.

I always dreamed of playing with the Yankees or Giants. Babe Ruth was my hero. I used to dream of hitting home runs into the friendly right-field stands in the Yankee Stadium or Polo Grounds.

Why, I had followed baseball since I was old enough to read and the Red Sox had been mired in the second division throughout my boyhood.[2]

*His opinion of what really happened the day he was farmed out to
Minneapolis in 1938, after he couldn't break into the outfield of
Joe Vosmik, Doc Cramer, and Sam Chapman:*

While walking to the bus, I was accompanied by Johnny
Orlando, the Red Sox clubhouse man who later became a
very good friend of mine. Before we parted, I turned to Johnny
and remarked, "Those guys, Cramer, Vosmik, and Chapman,
think I'm a pretty fresh kid. And they've got the laugh on me
now. But don't worry, I'll be back here next spring. And before
I get through I'm going to make a bigger salary for one year
than those three outfielders combined."[3]

*His immediate opinion upon losing out, after batting .406, to Joe
DiMaggio for the 1941 American League most valuable player
award:*

Well, a good man got it, anyhow.[4]

*His instant opinion on being pulled from a game by manager Joe
Cronin for loafing at the plate and in the field in 1942:*

I guess I was just kind of unconscious out there. I was too
lackadaisical. I was going to take three strikes down the gut.
Then I decided to try to hit a few line drives at those wolves
in left field.

I know it was my fault and Joe did the right thing in
taking me out of the game. I'm just thick-headed enough,

screwy enough and childish enough to let those wolves in left field get under my skin. Someday I'm going to bring 25 pounds of raw hamburger out there and invite those wolves down to enjoy it.[5]

His opinion of young fans:

There's just one group I don't think I would be able to take a riding from. That's the kids. I've always done everything I could for kids because I remember how I was once. I've never refused a kid an autograph in my life. I try to slip them old balls and bats every chance I get. If a middle-aged man boos me, I just feel sorry for him because I think he ought to know better. But if the kids, even though I realize they might be ignorant of the facts, start to get on me, I'm afraid that might be a little too tough to take.[6]

His opinion of military service, offered from Pensacola, Florida, where he underwent advance flight training during World War II:

This taking orders isn't exactly what I go for. But pretty soon I'll have a stripe or a bar, and maybe I can give a few orders myself.

They let us elect the branch we want to go into. We don't actually choose it—that's up to them—but we can tell them what we want to do.

I put down "Marine fighter" first, and let the other choices just string down. Some of my buddies are in the Marines, and

anyway I like the idea of being alone up there, with nobody to
worry about but myself.[7]

His opinion, at age thirty-one, on when a ballplayer should retire:

I'm not going to stay in this game until I'm decrepit. I've seen
too many examples of players staying in the game too long. I
expect to be financially secure in a couple of years.

It's my contention that Babe Ruth and Lou Gehrig both
shortened their lives by playing too long. Gehrig was a fellow
who lived by the book. What was he? About 39 years old
when he died? The Babe, from what I hear, never heard of the
book. Yet he passed away much too young.

Both stayed in the game much longer than they should. If
you're going to quit, the time to quit is when you're at your
peak. Then the fans will have a better picture of you going out
in a blaze of glory. But if you stay around until your batting eye
has dimmed and your legs don't carry you around with their
youthful spring, that's the way most fans will remember you.
That's not for me.[8]

His opinion on the merits of bailing out of a blazing, crippled Pan-
ther jet during the Korean War:

It was pretty cramped. You had your life jacket, your life raft,
and you were sitting on your parachute. You didn't jump out.
You were blown out of the plane. I probably should have
bailed out. But I looked at my knees and I looked at the angle

I'd be coming out, and I figured I'd be leaving my kneecaps in that plane. That scared me to death.[9]

His opinion on how many times newspapermen misquoted him or took things out of context:

Hundreds. One day during a game, a harmless old codger who had taken one drink too many climbed over the railing and sauntered up to me in left field. "Ted," he said, "I just wanted to tell you that the fish are really biting at Cape Cod Canal." The cops ran out on the field and snapped him up. A photographer snapped him, too—with the cops holding his right arm. So next day the captions under the photo went something like this: "Fan tries to sock Williams in jaw." Those are the things that hurt.[10]

On what changed his opinion about retiring after the 1954 season:

This fellow walks up to me out of the blue in the Baltimore railroad station and tells me I can't quit. I was really depressed at the time—1954 was the year I had just come back from active service in Korea. Early in spring training, I had broken my collarbone, missed the first thirty-six games of the season, and didn't rack up enough times at bat to qualify for the batting championship. This fan in the station tells me why I can't quit: I owed it to baseball because I was within striking distance of all kinds of milestones—2,000 hits, 400 home runs, 1,500 runs batted in, etc. "You've got 1,930 hits

Ted holds up a pair of three-pound bass. He was a skillful and demanding fishing partner.

AP/WIDE WORLD PHOTOS

right now. You've got to come back next year and get to that 2,000 milestone."

Well, sir, that fellow knew more about me than I did. All I knew was how many home runs I had hit and what my batting averages were. This fellow—Ed Mifflin was his name—was in the upholstery business in Swarthmore, Pennsylvania. He spent a lot of time with me after that. Thanks to him, I decided to stay in baseball and my home run total, which would have only been 366 homers, rose to 521 at the end of 1960. Which put me third in that department behind Babe Ruth and Jimmie Foxx.[11]

His opinion on his tangles with fans and the press:

203

It's just that when fans and certain baseball writers abused me, I refused to roll over and play dead. Nobody nowadays accuses nightclub entertainers of feuding with audiences just because they have enough moxie to talk back to some rum-soaked heckler at a ringside table. I never feuded with anybody except a few dedicated Williams wallopers—professional scribes who for twenty years were busier figuring out my "persecution complex" than my batting average.[12]

His immediate opinion in 1948, when asked what the public reaction would be after his daughter was born while he was on a fishing trip. It took him five days to fly from Florida to Boston to visit his wife and new daughter:

To hell with that. They can't run my life.

I'm getting out of here as quick as I can. I'm going back to Florida as quick as I can.[13]

His opinion, at midcareer, on the Boston fans and sportswriters:

I don't give a damn about the fans. Most of them can go to hell. They don't bother me one damn bit. They've been on me for years, but I'm not worrying one bit. Let 'em boo all they want and let 'em cheer all they want. I'll ignore them just the same. If they get on me too much, I'm just hot-tempered enough to tell them exactly what I think of them.

The majority of fans are all right, but those bums in left field are just morons. They say I take offense too easily, but there isn't a man alive who could take all that filthy abuse those guys hand out without dishing some of it back.

The writers can go to hell, too. Not all. But most of them. They wail because I won't bother with them. Why should I, when all they're interested in is digging up dirt? They lurk behind pillars hoping to catch you in some wrong. Sportswriters today don't care about facts and figures. All they're interested in is your personal life. Give the fans records, scores, figures. That's what they want, not, "What does Joe Doakes have for breakfast in the morning?"[14]

His opinion, as a player, on tipping his cap:

No. Never. Why should I? After all that abuse they handed me? I don't ask anything of them and I won't give them anything. They boo me when I make an error, so why should I tip my cap when I hit a home run?

I'm still the same guy, ain't I? They can all go to hell. I'll never tip my cap to them.

It doesn't pay to be nice. Look at Jimmie Foxx, as nice a guy who ever swung a bat. He tipped his hat to everybody. He waved to the fans. He was the life of every party.

Look at him today. Baseball has forgotten about him. No, it doesn't pay to be nice.[15]

His opinion on not shaking hands with teammates at home plate:

In his first year of retirement, Ted poses with a big one that did not get away—a 557-pound bluefin tuna that he landed off Rhode Island. Ted would willingly supply his opinion on fishing and just about anything else.

I don't believe in it. That's a silly practice and it doesn't mean a thing. Some do it just to put a show on for the fans. If a fellow hits a home run, I let him know how I feel about it in the dugout, but no hand shaking for me.

Stephens used to shake my hand all the time after I hit a home run, but I told him to cut it out. The other day, he told me that since he stopped shaking hands with me, he's gotten a hundred letters from people calling him a conceited, jealous so-and-so because he refuses to shake hands with me.[16]

His opinion of criticism that he didn't hustle:

I always try to do my best in a ballgame. Why, then, do some writers call me a man who doesn't play for the team? I have been accused of loafing in the outfield and on the bases. Maybe it looks that way to some people, but that's because of my lanky frame and because I run with a loping stride. I'm not so graceful as other players, but I always hustle and I have no use for anybody who doesn't.

It gripes me when some writers say I don't hit in the clutch. That's a lot of rot. Any guy who drives in over a hundred runs, scores over a hundred runs, and hits over .300 year after year, must win more than his share of games. I don't care who he is.

I've got one major fault. When things go badly, I get down. I guess that's one of the reasons I got off to such a bad start with the newspapermen in Boston. I was so tense and eager to make good, that when things didn't break my way, I couldn't take it in stride.[17]

His opinion on his right to spit, after several saliva outbreaks in 1956:

I'm going to continue to give it to those characters. Nobody's going to make me stop spitting. The newspaper guys in this town are bush. And some of those fans are the worst in the world. What do they want from a guy? I've hit .330 for seventeen years in this league and every time I walk up there, they give me the business. What do you expect me to do? Smile at them?[18]

His opinion, shortly after his retirement, on how to improve baseball:

You know, I'd like to see them try something I've been thinking about for three or four years. It's drastic and might never be taken seriously. But times and conditions change, and I'm wondering why they couldn't try it during spring training, when games don't mean anything.

It's this: instead of giving a batter four balls and three strikes, why not cut down to three balls and two strikes? In other words, he walks on the third ball or is out on the second strike.

I realize it's tampering with one of the oldest rules in the book, but think about it for a minute. It has interesting possibilities. Everybody's complaining about the length of games, but a shorter ball-and-strike count might cut as much as thirty minutes off playing time. It would help keep pitchers strong and bring more complete games. They wouldn't have to change pitchers as often as they do now.

Of course it would put more pressure on the hitter, because you'd be taking one swing away from him. But he would make up his mind quicker. I often took a strike or two, knowing I still had the third one left. If a hitter knew he only had two swings, he would be more alert. A lot of hitters get lazy up there.[19]

His opinion on fishing in Florida in the off-season:

These Everglades are right down my alley. I get all the fishing I want, and there's nobody here to bother me. There aren't more than 250 people in this town and that suits me fine. No cars. No buses, no noise. It's a pleasure to be away from that rat-race in cities.[20]

His opinion of the Atlantic salmon:

The Atlantic salmon is very romantic, very edible, and anything else good you can say about a fish. They're magnificent. I suppose if I had one fish to fish for the rest of my life, it would be the Atlantic salmon.[21]

His opinion on whether, as manager of the Washington Senators, he could get along with a cantankerous player like Ted Williams:

If he can hit like Ted Williams, yes.[22]

His opinion of the ideal manager:

Leo Durocher's a great manager and every leader has to have a hunk of Durocher in him. But to me the complete manager— my idol as a handler of men as opposed to a man-handler— was Joe McCarthy, my mentor on the Boston Red Sox. I've never wanted to please anyone in my life as much as I wanted to please him.

He inspired and instilled a real businesslike attitude toward baseball in me and all twenty-five men on the team. He made us feel that every tick of the clock on the baseball field was a golden moment which must not be allowed to slip by. And he never took a piece out of our hide.[23]

His opinion of his new job, fifty-five games into his managerial career with the Washington Senators:

I can't honestly tell you that I love managing. I like being on the field. I like being with the players and talking with them about their problems. I love talking about hitting and pitching. I love the game while we are playing it. I love the sixth, seventh, eighth and ninth innings.

I hate all the dinners. I hate all the television interviews and I hate having all the writers on your neck.[24]

His opinion on the joys of managing, during his third year with the Washington Senators:

I am only here to get enough money to do what I really like. I have expensive tastes. I read books on where to go hunt and fish. I know the price of plane tickets and I know how much it costs to stay in the best places.

I'd take off for a place in Kenya that has never been hunted. I'd come out of there with a 120-pound elephant. When you say a 120-pound elephant you are talking about the tusks. That's how the size of an elephant is measured.[25]

His opinion of hitters who appear "good and relaxed" at the plate:

Good and relaxed! That's just the way you're not supposed to be up there. You've got to be coiled like a snake ready to spring. You can't be relaxed. Did I look relaxed when I played?[26]

A dream, in his opinion not a nightmare, he had while being treated for the effects of a stroke in 1994:

I was in the hospital, the tubes in me, in a bed that's too short. I'm half asleep. I dream I'm in spring training working with the young Red Sox hitters like I did for years. But somehow Randy Johnson is out there on the mound, the big left-hander with Seattle that the guy on the Phillies bailed out on in the All-Star game last year. John Kruk wanted no part of that big left-hander.

Now with Johnson out there, all the Red Sox kids are saying, "Why don't you go up there and take a few cuts?"

I tell them, "I haven't hit in years and I just had a stroke and I can't see too well," but they keep teasing me and I say, "Yeah, I'll do it." But as I'm walking to home plate, I'm thinking, "I'm not going to try to pull this guy because he can really throw." The first pitch, he laid one right in there. I pushed at it. Line drive through the box for a base hit.[27]

His opinion of political columnist George Will as a baseball writer, as told to Will:

I'm a big fan of yours, a b-i-g fan. But George, you don't know a thing about baseball.

You wrote in one of your books that I used to take a pitch an inch outside for a walk when a hit might have knocked in a key run. The problem with that, George, is suppose I'd have swung at a pitch an inch outside, what about the pitch one inch inside? If I swing at that, how about the pitch an inch too high, or an inch too low? And why stop at an inch? How about two inches? George, if I'da hit the way you wanted me to, instead of being a .340 hitter, I'da hit .240.[28]

His opinion on death:

I've never been very religious, so I don't know what's going to happen, if anything, when I'm dead. I'll tell you this, though, I'm not afraid to die.[29]

APPENDIX
NOTES
INDEX

THEODORE SAMUEL "TED" WILLIAMS

The Kid, The Thumper, The Splendid Splinter

Born: August 30, 1918
Bats left, throws right
6'3" 205 lbs.
MLB Debut: April 20, 1939
Elected to the Hall of Fame: 1966

YEAR	TEAM	G	AB	R	H	2B	3B	HR	RBI	BB	SO	AVG
1939	Bos	149	565	131	185	44	11	31	**145**	107	64	.327
1940	Bos	144	561	**134**	193	43	14	23	113	96	54	.344
1941	Bos	143	456	**135**	185	33	3	**37**	120	**145**	27	**.406**
1942	Bos	150	522	**141**	186	34	5	**36**	**137**	**145**	51	**.356**
1946	Bos	150	514	**142**	176	37	8	38	123	**156**	44	.342
1947	Bos	156	528	**125**	181	40	9	**32**	**114**	**162**	47	**.343**
1948	Bos	137	509	124	188	**44**	3	25	127	**126**	41	**.369**
1949	Bos	155	566	**150**	194	**39**	3	**43**	**159**	**162**	48	.343
1950	Bos	89	334	82	106	24	1	28	97	82	21	.317
1951	Bos	148	531	109	169	28	4	30	126	**144**	45	.318
1952	Bos	6	10	2	4	0	1	1	3	2	2	.400
1953	Bos	37	91	17	37	6	0	13	34	19	10	.407
1954	Bos	117	386	93	133	23	1	29	89	**136**	32	**.345**
1955	Bos	98	320	77	114	21	3	28	83	91	24	.356
1956	Bos	136	400	71	138	28	2	24	82	102	39	.345
1957	Bos	132	420	96	163	28	1	38	87	119	43	**.388**
1958	Bos	129	411	81	135	23	2	26	85	98	49	**.328**
1959	Bos	103	272	32	69	15	0	10	43	52	17	.254
1960	Bos	113	310	56	98	15	0	29	72	75	41	.316
TOTAL		2292	7706	1798	2654	525	71	521	1839	2019	709	.344

Boldface = Led league

NOTES

Chapter 1: Thumping Theodore

1. Donald Honig, *Baseball When the Grass Was Real* (New York: Coward, McCann & Geoghegan, 1975), 119–20.
2. Interview with the author for the *Boston Herald*, 1991.
3. *Boston Record*, 16 January 1958.
4. *Boston Herald*, 30 January 1966.

Chapter 2: Teddy Ballgame

1. Donald Honig, *Baseball Between the Lines* (New York: Coward, McCann & Geoghegan, 1975), 40–41.
2. *Boston Herald*, 2 April 1957.
3. *Boston American*, 14 January 1959.
4. *Boston American*, 14 January 1958.
5. *Boston Record*, 16 January 1958.
6. *Boston American*, 15 January 1958.

7. *Boston Herald*, 13 January 1958.

8. Interview with the author for the *Boston Herald*, 1991.

Chapter 3: Two Teds

1. *Boston Herald*, 8 September 1946.

2. *Boston Herald*, 9 April 1939.

3. *Boston American*, 10 January 1958.

4. *Boston American*, 9 January 1958.

5. *Boston American*, 8 January 1958.

6. Ibid.

7. *Boston American*, 22 January 1958.

8. *Boston Herald*, 21 January 1958.

9. Associated Press, 19 June 1950.

10. Interview with the author for the *Boston Herald*, 1988.

Chapter 4: Terrible Ted

1. Ed Linn, *Hitter* (San Diego: Harvest, 1993), 136–37.

2. *Boston Sunday Advertiser*, 23 January 1966.

3. Interview with the author for the *Boston Herald*, 1989.

4. *New York Times*, 9 November 2000.

Chapter 5: Ted Afield

1. *Boston Herald*, 12 June 1946.

Chapter 6: Ted's Opinion

1. *Boston Herald*, 7 September 1941.

2. *Boston Herald*, 24 June 1950.

3. *Saturday Evening Post*, 21 April 1954.

4. *Boston Post*, 16 November 1941.

5. *Boston Herald*, 2 July 1942.

6. *Boston American*, 1 April 1942.

7. *Boston Herald*, 28 December 1943.

8. *Boston Herald*, 27 June 1950.

9. Interview with the author for the *Boston Herald*, 24 May 1997.

10. *Boston Herald*, 27 April 1969.

11. Ibid.

12. Ibid.

13. *Boston Herald*, 2 February 1948.

14. *Boston Herald*, 20 June 1950.

15. *Boston Herald*, 21 June 1950.

16. *Boston Herald*, 22 June 1950

17. *Saturday Evening Post*, 21 April 1954.

18. *Boston Herald*, 21 July 1956.

19. *Christian Science Monitor*, 24 July 1964.

20. United Press, 22 February 1949.

21. *Boston Traveler*, 23 June 1967.

22. *Boston Globe*, 22 February 1969.

23. *Boston Herald*, 27 April 1969.

24. *Boston Herald*, 7 June 1969.

25. *Boston American*, 4 March 1971.

26. *Boston Herald*, 5 October 1969.

27. *New York Times*, 22 May 1994.

28. *New York Times*, 9 November 2000.

29. Ibid.

INDEX

ABOUT THE AUTHOR

David Cataneo is a former baseball columnist, editor, and award-winning reporter for the *Boston Herald*. His previous books include *I Remember Joe DiMaggio*, *Peanuts and Crackerjack*, *Hornsby Hit One Over My Head*, and *Tony C*, a finalist for the 1997 Casey Award for best baseball book.